Her Shallow Grave

Betty, I did the best job I could to preserve your memory and I hope this is what you wanted. May your story just like you never be forgotten- your friend always... Matina

Daddy, I miss you and I always will, love doesn't end with death. I only wish you could be here reading this... Tia

Chapters

PREFACE

The purpose of this book has never been about money or recognition it has been about the life and innocence stolen from a young girl.

What makes a crime one that will always be remembered? Is it the brutality, or how close to home it occurred, how about how it stole the trust of the community and changed how people live? This is the story that would meet this definition.

I have tried to stick to facts as much as possible that I found in court transcripts, interviews I have conducted, articles and newspaper reports.

I hope this book will help answer questions surrounding the circumstances of the murder of Betty Jean Necessary and possibly help other families that have lost a family member. Although this crime happened several years ago, it will never be forgotten and Betty's short life need not be forgotten.

I admire Betty's family a great deal since they continued to make sure Fred Bowen stayed in prison where he belonged until he died. Without their vigilant awareness of what was going on with him, he would have gotten out of prison, where he could resume to hurt again since Fred was a serial killer.

Betty and her family lived close to my grandparents in a small suburb called Bloomingdale which was about 10 miles from where I grew up in Church Hill, Tennessee. The local newspaper, Kingsport Times News reported on Betty Necessary who had disappeared from the road, she walked every day to school with her sister and two neighborhood friends on February 26, 1970. After searching for two days the body of 12 year old Betty Necessary was found in a small cave not far from her home. My aunt was working as a nurse at Holston Valley Hospital when Betty's body was brought in. My aunt told me how several doctors and nurses came from all floors of the hospital to see the broken body of the 12 year old girl. Comments were made about how they couldn't believe that only one man did this much damage to her it had to have been the work of at least two men- two monsters at that. Even when the police said it was only one man I discovered the popular opinion of those that I interviewed in the community believed it was the work of at least two men.

One man interviewed for the murder later admitted to anybody that would listen that he was also responsible. He was warned so much to quit scaring other people around him, he was thrown out of a store and a mobile home park where he lived and asked to never come back. This could have been the bragging of somebody that just wanted to talk about a crime he had nothing to do with and again the information he was providing was accurate.

The Necessary murder shocked so many residents that well-meaning adults kept warning the girls about what had happened and to not trust anybody- to always travel in groups or at least one other person. It's difficult not feeling safe and not doing anything about it.

I was a small child, only 6 years old and probably the reason I knew as much as I did was because my grandparents and some of my relatives lived in Bloomingdale. I kept on hearing about how this could have been any of us girls and he could have done this to us while we visited with our grandparents in Bloomingdale which was at least weekly visits. I kept seeing visions of Betty being hurt and killed and couldn't get this off my mind- to know that she was so innocent and could do nothing to protect herself. Not only was I trying to deal with the potential to get hurt by a madman, but my grandmother in Church Hill was dying of breast cancer, so I was watching how a silent killer was taking away my beloved grandmother I loved so much.

It was impossible to fall asleep at night because the images in my mind and the information I was hearing from relatives would replay at night. I had a cousin that went to school with Betty and some relatives that went to school and knew Bowen's relatives. It is hard for me to stress how bad this affected me and when I tried to talk about this to anybody I was told not to talk or think about it. The consequences of being a sensitive child were taking its toll. Whether it was exhaustion or truly an experience that doesn't happen often, I can only tell you I believe and nothing or nobody will ever change my mind on the visit I shared one night with Betty Jean Necessary who beyond her own death cared enough to visit and let me know that she was okay, that life existed on the other side that had repaired her in her own words "better than new".

During one particularly long day, I went to bed and pretended to sleep as usual with the blanket up over my head when I sensed something in my room. Although hard to explain, I was not scared, but felt like somebody I knew well was in the room with me. After slowly pulling the covers down, I saw a child in a pale pink dress that looked like an angel dancing in my room- she was dancing in circles and a warm glow surrounded her. I knew immediately who the girl was and I didn't have to ask - it was Betty Necessary. I wasn't scared which is strange but I was almost relieved to see her. Betty and I had a conversation that only children can have and she told me I didn't need to worry about her anymore since she had been fixed back better than new and twirled around to show me how pretty she looked. There was nothing like I had been told before about blood on her, her skin was white just like porcelain, her hair was not matted or dirty but clean and just like silk.

I asked her about what happened and if she hurt for long, Betty told me I didn't need to worry about that because it was all over with and done- she wasn't hurting anymore. I understood what she was saying when she told me I needed to quit worrying about her.

She told me when she left the earth three angels fixed her back good as new and then took her to heaven where she didn't hurt anymore and was never hungry, she was happy all the time. She said there wasn't anything ugly or scary where she was at and she was back to the way she was before and I didn't need to be afraid, it was okay.

Betty told me I needed to eat, sleep well and get my education- it was very important to grow up because one of these days she would need me to help her, but right now I just needed to get strong and get big- I had to grow up. Strange as it sounds I knew exactly what she was talking about.

She told me she would let me know when I needed to help her and not to worry when it would be I would just know it; she would make sure that I knew the time was right. Betty started to hum and sing "Amazing Grace" which I recognized from church and fell asleep not long after she sang. To this day I have never heard a more beautiful voice than the one I heard the night I met Betty. I never doubted my visit with her and I never shared it because it was a special visit just between the two of us.

I slept better that night than what I had slept in many weeks and woke up to feel better. After this visit I didn't think of Betty like I had before and I knew I had a purpose in my life, I was here to help Betty but didn't know how at the time- I would know later and I was okay with that.

Through the years when petitions came around for Fred Bowen's release from prison I promptly signed everyone I could and urged others to do so.

Years later, after I had gotten married and had a life of my own, my husband and I attended a dinner party where I was introduced to a couple from the Bloomingdale community. The couple that was there brought up the crime of how Betty had been killed and how they believed it was about time again for Fred Bowen to get out of prison. The whole topic of the brutal murder resurfaced for a reason. The same couple said it was a shame because if he got out he would do it again and a bigger shame because he wasn't the only one involved in the murder. The room took on a different look, the lighting flickered and the tone was altogether changed. I had no doubt and knew immediately that Betty was nudging me, letting me know that she needed me to help her and that it was time to tell her story.

Even though my relatives had moved out of Bloomingdale it was time to go back to 1970, to the small community of Bloomingdale and to the small cave where the body of a 12 year old child was found after being shot several times, brutally raped, and buried alive to die alone.

Her Only Fear

There is nothing in this world that Betty was more scared of or dreaded more than walking up the road that led through the woods to her home by herself. Betty wasn't scared of anything unless it came to the area at the top of the hill on Kingsley Avenue, where the road curved and led through a long wooded section of graveled road to her home. Trees and thick brush lined each side of the road making it difficult to see into the woods- which has been always dark and ominous. Friends and family would often tease her which would leave her dreading the trip even more because she didn't like being made fun of. Betty walked to school with Joyce and Wanda Hickman every day and normally her older sister Teresa walked with them as well; however, Teresa was at home sick with the flu and was not with her.

Wanda and Joyce also lived on Kingsley Avenue but their house was in the lower section of the road and Betty lived at the very top of Kingsley Avenue what is now Crystal View. Betty asked Wanda and Joyce to walk her home because of the uneasy feelings she had; however, they had already made plans to go to town with a neighbor so they couldn't walk with her. After she dropped the Hickman girls off, she stayed only for a few minutes at their house to see their new baby niece brought home from the hospital that day.

Betty started off on her walk and Wanda stood outside and told her she would watch her walk to the top of the hill and reminded her it was only a short distance once you got to the top of the hill to where Betty lived. There was a curve to the left as you crested the top of Kingsley Avenue and a small stretch of road about 400-500 feet which led to Betty's house. The small stretch of woods was the section that Betty dreaded and feared the most. This is where she had seen something in the woods and it made her scared beyond comprehension. It had only been a few months before when she mentioned to a friend she feared that area because that was a bad place, she had seen people hiding in that section of the woods. Since they knew that she feared that area they felt like she was her imagination that had caused her to see something.

The last time that Wanda seen Betty was when she got to the top of Kingsley Avenue and Betty turned around to waive bye to her and also perhaps to indicate that she was okay. Betty then turned back around and walked around the curve through the wooded area of roadway which put her out of sight. There was a small white house at the end of this section; however the couple that lived in the house was gone through the week and it was occupied only on the weekends when the husband was home. Since this was a Thursday the house was empty because the wife stayed with family during the week.

As Betty walked, she tried to fill her mind with good thoughts; however, she could not shake the feeling she was being watched and had been feeling the watchful eyes for several days.

February 26, 1970 was a typical East Tennessee day which meant it was moderately cold, damp and once the sun went down got cooler. The urge to run through the woods was something that Betty fought with every day. Betty was not a weak girl, she could compete with any boy at running or softball since she had brothers and was used to playing with them; she was a great natural athlete. The only way to get past the fears about where she was at was to think good thoughts so she filled her mind with the baby she had just seen in the Hickman house and how cute she was sweet and she smelled. She felt bad because she had taken the time to stop by and see the new baby but knew her mom and dad would understand.

Betty's parents were strict and they normally wanted their children home right after school, everybody had chores to do. Betty knew she had to be at home on time today since the entire family had the flu and they were relying on her to fix the meals. So many thoughts filled her mind as she walked, things she needed to do when she got home, things she wanted to do, but still the dread of her walk was the most prominent thing occupying her thoughts.

Betty could sing beautifully and had a desire and love of music like no other. Music had always been a source of comfort for her and she began to silently sing to herself. Fear knotted her stomach and a funny taste appeared in her mouth for no reason; she needed to stay in the middle of the road not too far one way or the other. She smelled the air and thought to herself that it wouldn't be long before spring was here and she looked forward to it.

Betty clutched her school books to her chest and kept on walking while the man who appeared suddenly tried to make conversation with her.

The man that approached Betty was one she was familiar with and had no real fear of, so when he talked to her she was not surprised by him. He was not alone, which Betty discovered, but it was far too late. A swing of the butt of a gun is all that it takes to render a small girl compliant and she was quickly taken from the roadway by her abductors.

The area she was so scared of swallowed her up and took her away on February 26, 1970.

Betty Necessary

Betty Jean Necessary was the youngest daughter of Walter and Dorothy Hartsock Necessary: she was born at Holston Valley Hospital on September 15, 1957. Although she was a lithe young woman she was still a child. Betty was described by friends as shy, but friendly and had the voice of an angel; she also had an infectious laugh. Typical of teenagers of that day she loved dancing, bubble gum, running and eating- she just loved life.

The Necessary's was a very poor family but they were very proud and did the best they could with what earnings they had. It wasn't uncommon for them to wear hand-me-down's from friends or family members. Raising a family is hard but when limited on money it is even harder and it wasn't uncommon for the kids in their family to be made fun of. Betty never let anybody see the jokes hurt her because she knew kids could be cruel and she knew what the important things in life were.

Some have said that Mr. Necessary made his mistakes in life, but the one thing he was proud of is that he saw the error of his ways and had become a religious person. I guess because Walter

Necessary had seen some unpleasant things in life he raised his children in a very strict fashion and both the boys and the girls knew that when it was time to come home they better be home and they better always listen to their parents.

Betty's friends couldn't understand the extent of strictness in Betty's parents and they would sometimes be persuaded to go home with her to beg her parents to let her attend a sock hop, ball game or even a sleep over but it was so rarely granted most of the time they wouldn't even ask her parents.

Animals were something that Betty loved and it wasn't unusual for her to be carrying around a cat, dog or bunny. Betty had a cat that loved that her so much that when she disappeared the cat also disappeared, never to be seen again- some believe that the cat mourned itself to death.

Betty rode horses when she was younger and was an excellent rider, maybe given more time she might have been more accomplished with horses.

Growing up in a family of several boys Betty learned how to play hard and she could crack a baseball or softball and run as good if not better as any boy. The one thing you could say about Betty is that she was well loved and she loved life. Being easily embarrassed about boys she was often teased by family and friends that would say she had a boyfriend and she would quickly correct them.

Depending on what perspective you are talking about 12 years is a long time or a short time, for Betty it was all the time she had and it was too short. Although Betty had a short life, she had more friends and people that loved her and had faith in her than Freddie Bowen or the other killers involved would ever have in their lifetimes.

Fred Bowen

Fred J. Bowen was born on April 23, 1944 in St. Charles, Virginia. His mother was Myrtle Fritz Bowen and his father was Charlie Roberts. Since his mother and father were not married he was given the Bowen name. When Fred was around 8 years old, his adult half- brother Andrew, who lived in Kingsport picked Fred and Myrtle up in Virginia and brought them back with him to Kingsport to help take care of both of them. Andrew had a family of his own, one still at home so he had a lot of responsibilities. Andrew had a business called the Bloomingdale Grill, which kept him busy and several locals would eat there.

The Bloomingdale Grill served decent food that also had pinball machines and pool tables; it was well known that a little gambling took place there too. Andrew's family helped him run the place and they all took their turns in waiting tables and cooking. Fred never helped Andrew much with anything and was more of a family misfit than anything but Andrew tried to do what he thought was best by his mother, but with a family of his own he could only do so much and if you ever met Fred you could easily see where anybody had their limitations with him.

Although Fred never helped Andrew in the grill he was there and was a fixture just as much as the pinball machines and pool tables. The regulars knew him and knew to avoid him when he was there because he didn't have good sense.

Teachers at Kingsley Elementary School tried their best with Fred but like everything else only so much could be done with him. Kingsley Elementary had a small staff and they couldn't keep their eyes on him all the time.

Fred's mother didn't try hard to discipline him and it soon became clear in the Bloomingdale community that Freddie did what he wanted to do, he stole from other kids or beat up on them, and hurt animals, for Freddie Bowen there was no limits to what he would do. The best thing to do when you see him was to pretend you didn't see him and walk the other way.

When he was in the sixth grade much to the delight of fellow students and teachers Fred decided to quit school. I don't think anybody enforced or followed up with getting Fred back into school since most were glad he was gone.

Most students know how to read and write by the time they have reached the sixth grade, however Fred never learned to do either. By his own admission, Fred could recognize small words he had memorized so due to his educational limitations, he would always have problems in earning a living.

Not long after Fred quit school his brush with the law began. A list of some arrests on record was breaking and entering in 1963, criminal registration in 1964, drunk driving in 1966, documented premeditated rape/contributing to the delinquency of a minor in 1967 and a smaller violation of registration laws/driving without a license in 1968. By most accounts, Fred was the person that stayed to himself most of the time, more of a loner. You would see him either walking or riding a bike that was most likely stolen.

At the time of the Necessary murder, both Fred and his brother in law Phillip Laforce were under investigation for burglary at Kingsley Elementary School.

Not surprising, Fred's legal counsel tried to explain previous head injuries as the source of his problems. Fred had a bicycle wreck when he was younger and flew across the handlebars of the bike hitting his head; he also had a car accident where he hit his head on the roof of the car. These were injuries he had sustained as a juvenile and no records could be found where he had been treated at a local hospital for the injuries. He also fell down a 22 step staircase while employed at a former job in Indiana as an adult and claimed he had sustained injuries from the fall.

Fred had tried his hand at house painting, restaurant work, custodial work and he admitted he never spent over 90 days at a job. Like a lot of men his age, Fred learned how to make a living by using his wits and sold items he could get his hands on which usually meant what he stole from other people. Although Fred told the police when interviewed that he had traded and sold items you have to wonder if part what he had was stolen goods, especially since a lot of the things he had was diamonds and jewelry sets. Fred was also a decent gambler and made a little money by gambling, either by true skill or cheating.

Fred had been staying between Kingsport and Indiana since the late 1960's because he had family in both locations, but he had traveled to other states such as California and Florida by thumbing a ride which used to be a very popular mode of transportation especially for men.

Fred was not a bad looking man and not intimidating. At the time of his arrest, he weighed 150 pounds and was 6'1" inches tall, his rugged features complimented his blue eyes and brown hair. Sometimes he would be in need of a shave or haircut, but let's face it, that describes a lot of men.

It wasn't unusual for Fred to travel since he could do trading and selling of his wares which included not only diamonds and jewelry sets but also guns and knives.

Fred had been married twice and was married to Sandra Louise Laforce Bowen when he was arrested. They had been married about 18 months when he was arrested and had no children.

Chadwell Road

Chadwell Road is a feeder road which runs about 3 miles and is assessable by either Wadlow Gap Road or Bloomingdale Road. It is dotted on each side with residences, pasture land and at least one dried up pond formerly used for cattle. One small road that at first looks like a washed out forgotten driveway is really a hidden road that leads to some of the prettiest land in the Bloomingdale area. In the spring the lush green rolling fields are alive with wild dogwood and Redbud trees full with blooms. A short walk will take you to an area that leads down to a gully thick with wildflowers, ferns and moss.

When I toured the property back in 2009 it had changed a lot since 1970 but some things had changed little.

A gully is hidden within the rolling hillsides and a natural depression in the earth that at first seems to be a small non-descript area but upon closer inspection will reveal an empty tomb. The tomb I speak about is the cave that 12 year old Betty Necessary was left to die after she had been raped and shot several times. It is cold, damp, scary and small not being a size you think a 12 year old body could fit into. Through the years since 1970 this cave has been filled in to hide its secret and keep nosy individuals from finding it, but this cave refuses to be hidden it wants its secret to be known. You can almost feel the regret it feels it played in this crime.

There are so many Forget Me Not flowers that blanket the gulley and cave area to cover the past and make it pretty.

Even though some things have changed since 1970 for Chadwell Road the one thing that remains unchanged is the part Chadwell Road played in Betty Necessary's murder. Had it not been for the altercation in the middle Chadwell Road on the evening of February 26, 1970 the murder of Betty Necessary would not have been so prompt and probably her killer, at least one of them might have been on his way back to Indiana to evade arrest.

One of the families that lived on Chadwell Road was Carl and Lucille Laforce and they had lived on Chadwell Road for several years while raising their children. Lucille's mother, Rose Dunn also lived on Chadwell Road and was only a short distance from Lucille and Carl.

Sandra Laforce Bowen was one of the grown children of Carl and Lucille she had been married to Fred Bowen for about 18 months. Fred and Sandra had come in for a visit from Indiana where they had been living for several months. Space was limited at the Laforce house so Fred had been staying with Rose Dunn, along with Phil Laforce who was Sandra's grown brother. Phil normally lived with his grandmother so this was home to him.

Fred stayed at the Dunn home except for the few nights he had stayed with his half-brother Andrew who lived on Bloomingdale Road. Fred and Sandra had made plans initially to return to Indiana the weekend before February 26th but for some unknown reason had stayed a little longer.

Fred Bowen didn't have a good reputation and was known around Bloomingdale as trouble, he had been in jail before, was known to steal and fight.

On the night of February 26, 1970, one of the neighbors heard an argument looked out in the roadway where the noise was coming from to see Fred, Sandra and Phil walking down the roadway while fighting. The neighbor knew Fred's reputation, so they called the police and the man of the house came to the door and told them to quiet it down. The argument between Fred and Sandra then switched to Fred and the neighbor, and Fred threatened the neighbor. Fred was finally persuaded by Phillip to leave before the police showed up. The police were called and the altercation was reported, this turned out to be what prompted police to investigate Fred and Phillip in the murder of Betty Necessary.

Fred, Sandra and Phillip continued to walk down the road toward the direction of the Dunn and Laforce houses and by the time they got there everything had settled down. When finally they reached their destination Sandra remained at her mom and dad's house while both Fred and Phillip stayed with Rose Dunn. This had been the arrangement since they arrived in Kingsport so this was not unusual.

Since the police had been called to the location of Chadwell Road due to the complaints of arguing a door to door questioning took place by the police and the residents on Chadwell Road were questioned to see who had heard any part of the disturbance. Although the police showed up at the Laforce and Dunn homes that night to discuss the disturbance everything by then everything had settled down and the police left satisfied for the moment it was finally quiet.

Fred was questioned that night and he admitted to getting mad and arguing with his wife and a neighbor. He apologized to the police and told them it wouldn't happen again.

I'm sure the police thought by showing up and making an appearance this showed the young couple they needed to solve their problems by talking things out rather than arguing and disturbing everybody.

Little did the police know that night how close they were to a killer and to solving another crime far more important than a disturbance from a bickering married couple.

The Search

When Betty didn't show up on time her mother, Dorothy

Necessary was not alarmed since it was common for Betty Jean to

stay at the Hickman home and eat supper with them. She walked to

school with Wanda and Joyce Hickman every day and when school

was dismissed she walked home with them.

The one thing that Mrs. Necessary couldn't understand was Betty

knew the whole family was sick with the flu and it was not like her

to not come home right after school to help out. Betty was a very

mature, religious, young lady and took responsibility seriously.

After talking with a neighbor of the Hickman's, Mrs. Necessary

discovered the Hickman girls were going to town earlier with

another neighbor, so she assumed that Betty had gone to town with

them. Although Betty was a responsible young girl she was still

young and it was possible that she gave in to the temptation of

going downtown Kingsport with the other girls.

When 7:30 pm arrived the annoyance of Betty not showing up on

time morphed into fear and Mrs. Necessary called family. Besides

the children still living at home, the Necessary's had grown children, phone calls were made to verify Betty was not with them. Enough time had passed so concerned family and friends suggested it was time to call the police. Even if Betty went with the Hickman's to town the stores were now closed. Mrs. Necessary called the police and filed a report at 9:00 pm Thursday night. She spoke with Sheriff Bill Wright and his investigator John Bishop at 10:30 pm, after speaking with them the search for Betty was formally started.

In East Tennessee when a child is missing any volunteer who can will drop what they are doing and search as if that child were their own. Teams of volunteers from local law enforcement, rescue squads, fire department and neighbors searched immediately to find the young girl that disappeared into the area of the woods she had always feared. The search continued as long as daylight would allow and searchers only quit for the morning light.

Early the next morning teams searched the area where she was last seen and combed the hillsides of Bloomingdale all day. Kids at Kingsley Elementary School were questioned on Friday the 27th to see if they knew where Betty could be or if they had witnessed any suspicious activity. The only comment made out of the ordinary was when one schoolmate told the police that Betty had made an offhand comment two days before her disappearance she wanted to run away from home. When questioned more about the comment the schoolmate told the police there was no particular reason for her wanting to run away and she gave no reasons, just that she wanted to run away. A lot of kids this age make the same comment more of an expression of momentary displeasure so it was not taken seriously.

On Friday morning a tragic find was made while searching in the early afternoon on a steep slope about 100 yards from the gravel roadway where Betty disappeared. School books and papers that seemed to have been thrown in no particular order was found in the loose leaves of the gulley with a large adult footprint in the soft earth where somebody had stood at the rim of the gully and flung them. This was the first clue of what might have happened because whoever slung the papers and books did so as if the owner had no intention or reason to come back and pick them up. According to a neighborhood child a path led from the road where Betty disappeared to the gully where her books were found, but he doubted that Betty would have willingly gone down the path since she was so scared of the woods. One of the deputies told the other searchers to be careful and not contaminate the scene and he would go back and find the sheriff.

While the search for Betty was continued, her father commented to a reporter with the Kingsport Times Newspaper he believed she had been "snatched" since she had never stayed out all night before without calling them first. Mrs. Necessary also commented to a newspaper reporter about something that occurred the previous night before Betty went missing. According to Mrs. Necessary a carload of "drunk boys" in a Ford car had appeared on the road and talked to Betty and her sister Teresa and tried to get both the girls to get in the car with them. The newspaper did not identify who the boys were or indicate if the Necessary girls knew the boys.

A search of the area uncovered that a car had been driven up a muddy lane and left tracks that led from the direction of Chadwell Road and a small distance from the Necessary home. Casts were made of the impressions, however, it was pointed out the tracks could have been made by a searcher in their vehicle as well as the abductor. The tire tracks that led from Chadwell Road, went up a muddy lane, past an empty barn and up into the grass at the edge of the woods. No turnaround tracks were found so it was assumed that whoever had been driving had simply backed out or turned around in the thick grass. This area was so thickly covered with grass it would not leave a depression of a tire tread. Besides the tire tracks a single footprint was also found and an impression of the footprint was also made.

Due to the tire tracks coming from Chadwell Road and a police report called in on February 26th from a disturbance on Chadwell Road the investigators started a house by house search there and see if they could find out anything.

Normally this is not something that would have been mentioned but when the subject of missing Betty Necessary came up one of the deputy's brought up the strange coincidence of the disturbance on Chadwell Road the night before with TBI Special Agent James Keesling. On Friday, February 27th, Special Agent Keesling questioned Bowen about the disturbance.

Fred told the investigator he had been drinking on Thursday and Sandra did not like him drinking so the two had words and she took her purse and hit him over the eye putting a cut over his eye. Fred Bowen's name was not new to the police, but an argument between a married couple is common and both had seemed to have settled down since the argument occurred and was back to normal. Fred told the police he had learned his lesson and agreed to not drink anymore. Although things seemed to have settled down for Sandra and Fred, Special Agent Keesling commented after interviewing Bowen "there is something not right about that".

The search for Betty continued and it became a common sight to see searchers in orange clothing, walking up and down the hillsides on Kingsley Avenue and Chadwell Road to help locate the missing 12 year old. Two police dogs Satan and Apache were utilized to track and search the area help find the missing child but could find nothing.

The search on Friday yielded no results in finding Betty and children in the area were told by the police if they spotted any suspicious cars approach them to write down the tag number- if they had no pen handy to use a stick and write it in the dirt.

Relatives of the Necessary's in both Church Hill and Blountville were contacted and told that if they had heard anything from Betty to call Mr. and Mrs. Necessary as soon as possible. The search crews did their best and didn't stop except for a break to eat since she disappeared. It is no doubt they were tired and were growing weary but continued on from nothing but adrenaline. At the end of Friday, no results other than the school books were yielded and the search was stopped only due to lack of light.

Friends of Betty continued to pray and hope that Betty would be found safe and sound, but as time went by it became doubtful to everybody that she would.

Just as with Friday, the search continued on Saturday when the morning light came out to where the search crews could see. Shortly after dawn on Saturday some members out searching were fired upon about 4 or 5 times in the vicinity of the house where Fred Bowen had been staying while in Kingsport. The area was searched but nothing could be found that would explain the gun fire- some thought a car back firing was a possibility.

The hillsides in Bloomingdale are well known to be dotted with natural limestone formations and caves of different sizes. It only takes a little imagination to see how years of water flow have eroded the soft earth and rock into the little hideaway areas. Some of these caves are bigger than others and some have held garbage left by locals looking for a place to dump their trash, maybe even younger people who wanted to hide or have a party used them. Most of the area residents know where the caves are located since they are so common; some of the area children had played in these caves while growing up. Searchers were very careful to look in and around these caves.

Young boys and men who had hunted combed the woods and hillsides since someone with a knowledge of hunting would know the area better. About noon on Saturday, February 28th during the search of one of the cave areas a young boy spotted something and commented that the cave looked different, he had looked there earlier that day and he could see clearly into the cave. Now the appearance even from a distance seemed very different and you couldn't see into the cave, there was a definite obstruction. Small brush and branches that was not there earlier seemed to block the entrance of the cave.

Closer inspection revealed the reason for the "different appearance" of the cave and it also brought a sad end to the search for Betty Necessary. Beckoning hands with sticks between her fingers wrapped tightly as if she were beckoning for somebody to help her was the first thing the searchers seen. Many of the men, neighbors, emergency volunteers and police wept from the site. The small bullet ridden, bloody body of 12 year old Betty Jean Necessary was covered slightly with leaves, small branches and dirt in a makeshift grave that could be described as more of a depression in the earth.

The last futile attempts Betty made to free herself after being buried alive was visible.

Her body was naked except for part of the blouse which was still fastened; the collar of her blouse was almost torn off on one side and the sleeve was torn out on the other side. Her bra was torn down around the shoulders and hanging about her tightly bound hands. As more debris was raked back a dark coat which the child had on when she disappeared was discovered lying across her shoulders, partially buttoned. Several gunshots were observed in the back and front of the coat this was such a shocking sight that even well-seasoned law officers were sickened by the sight. Several layers of gags circled her head and were bound so tightly that it was later discovered at the autopsy there was also a wadded up gag in her mouth. This gag in her mouth had prevented blood that had filled Betty's lungs and throat from being expelled after she had been shot. Since Betty couldn't expel the blood it caused her to drown in her own blood.

Investigators searched and found articles of her clothing in a honeysuckle thicket about 200 yards from the cave and depressions in the tall grass indicated an assault had taken place there. Scuffle marks from human feet indicated an apparent struggle located around the mouth of the cave and sink hole led officers to speculate that Betty had fought very hard for her life. She saw the cave and where her attacker had been there earlier and dug her grave; she knew what would happen to her, but as much as she fought she couldn't avoid what was happening. It was theorized on the scene she was probably shot in the abdomen first and then lowered into the waiting grave and shot the additional times in her back since bullet holes in the coat indicate that she was shot after the coat was placed over her.

When Betty's body was found by the police, the body was carefully removed from the cave and carried by a makeshift stretcher to a Jeep that had to be utilized due to the rough terrain and then transported to an awaiting ambulance. Her body was taken immediately to the Holston Valley Community Hospital for an autopsy since they were the only medical facility equipped to handle autopsies at the time.

Later that day the Sheriff was questioned about the length of time Betty had been dead and he wouldn't answer. He commented that the body was found in an area that was inaccessible to her abductor by a car and the only way to get to the cave would be to cross over several barbed wire fences and heavy brush to get there. That is, unless there was an alternate route he didn't know about and possibly a better equipped vehicle was used that had been built for a rougher terrain- at this point it was only speculation.

Soil samples were taken from the cave where the body was found, the samples were placed in containers, sealed, identified and then mailed to the FBI laboratory in Washington, DC.

Due to the complexity of the case the TBI was called in to help with the investigation, which was common due to the manpower, training and expertise the TBI offered.

In 1970 the tools that police had to use were very limited and DNA was unheard of. Blood analysis and other tools we have today might shed more light on where the body had been before or after death.

The once beautiful, young, and vibrant Betty stopped being a person when she died and was evidence of a crime. For Betty help had arrived too late, but at least her family could grieve and give her a proper burial.

The Arrest of a Killer

The most important thing when a murder has occurred is to restore order and confidence to the public. The police needed to find out who committed this crime and put whoever was responsible for her murder behind bars. It hit home with everybody since this could have happened to anybody- it could have happened to one of their own children.

It was hard for residents that still left their doors open and unlocked to grasp what had happened to a young girl like Betty. Things like this did not happen in Kingsport, Tennessee.

One thing that the police were quick to determine is Betty's killer had to know about her routine and that she regularly walked the road with her sister but this time would be alone. One house faced the road which led through the woods where Betty disappeared; however, whoever abducted her knew the house was empty through the week. The man of the house worked out of town through the week and his wife stayed with relatives because she didn't want to be there alone.

Residents of the small community of Bloomingdale did not have to wait long and the arrest was probably what we could call record time. Although two other males had been taken into custody and several others questioned at length about the crime, it was the ruckus in the middle of Chadwell Road that occurred after Betty disappeared that led to the arrest of her killer. Investigators working the Necessary murder had been talking to police officers that had investigated a report on Thursday night regarding the disturbance on Chadwell Road between Fred Bowen and his wife Sandra. There was something about Fred's demeanor that wouldn't rest well with the investigators.

A great deal of questions came into the minds of investigators - could the argument that Fred and Sandra had on the 26th been more than a husband drinking too much?

One of the men picked up and questioned on Saturday, February 28th was Phillip Laforce; it was not revealed why Phillip was taken into custody, but while he was being questioned, he told police about a conversation with Fred on Thursday that piqued the interest of the detectives.

According to Phillip, Fred came by his grandmother's house to pick him up and discussed the day's events. Fred told Phillip he had shot somebody accidentally that day and told him about shooting into a bush and heard a cry. Upon investigating where the noise came from a body was discovered but Fred wouldn't tell Phillip whom had been killed. After Fred was finished with his story Phillip acted shocked as most people would. Fred laughed and told Phillip he was only kidding and accused him of believing everything and being too serious all the time.

While Phillip Laforce was still in custody Fred Bowen was arrested and then Phillip was released shortly after Fred was brought to the police station. When Fred was arrested, he offered no resistance, but kept repeating "I'm not going", he went and was booked into the jail. Both the Dunn and Laforce properties were thoroughly searched after Fred was arrested.

Fred admitted when he was booked that he had been at the police department before when he was charged with other crimes but couldn't recall the crimes.

After Fred was arrested a family member, Andrew Bowen which is Fred's brother contacted a local attorney who spoke with him while he was in custody. Although the attorney spoke with Fred briefly, he refused to represent him when he found out what he was being charged with. His only advice to Fred was not to talk to the police until he had legal representation.

The night of Fred's arrest, he was heard sobbing in his cell; why was he crying? Was it for himself was he thinking about how he had really messed up his life? There was no way he was sobbing for his victim.

News of what happened to Betty swept through Kingsport and Bloomingdale was in a rage. A group of residents was gathering up money to make Fred's bond so that when was released they had planned to kill him by hanging him and different groups had their own way they would carry this out. Unfortunately, he was never released to public and remained in solitary confinement for his own protection until his trial.

On Sunday everybody in Bloomingdale was talking about Freddie Bowen and how he had been in trouble with the law before, his reputation was not the greatest in the world, but this was something different. Fred was convicted of burglary twice in Sullivan County once in 1957 and again in 1963; picked up in Indianapolis, Indiana in 1967 for contributing to the delinquency of a minor girl but the charge was dropped when the parents dropped the charges. It was brought up later that more than likely this was a family member he tried to molest. Fred had been arrested for criminal registration violations in Miami, Florida, fined on two traffic charges in Kingsport, Tennessee and also picked up for misdemeanors with other cities. At the time of the murder of Betty Necessary, Fred was also being investigated for breaking into Kingsley Elementary School with his brother in law Phillip Laforce and stealing candy. Part of the candy and candy wrappers was found at the fence and outhouse when the residence of Rose Dunn was searched. Years ago an outhouse was common and anybody that has used one will tell you they are nasty, stink and can contain critters you don't want around you when you do your business. If the police would have searched the outhouse a little better they would probably have discovered something disposed of that would have been used in the murder of Betty Necessary.

The local newspapers reported daily just as they had been since Betty disappeared on what was happening with the investigation of her murder and Fred's arrest. Two Bloomingdale Gas Station attendants commented to Kingsport Times News that earlier in the week that Betty was killed a young man tried to sell them a gun matching the description of the gun used to kill Betty however nobody purchased it.

The gun used to kill Betty Jean Necessary was found Wednesday, March 4, 1970 after somebody called the police to tell them they seen somebody with Fred Bowen's description throw something in Chadwell Pond next to Chadwell Road and is about 1000 yards from Rose Dunn's house where Fred had been staying. The pond is about 2-3 feet deep and 50 feet across and had several feet of muck in the bottom. The gun was found with a large magnet tied to a boat; it was slightly rusted and had a charred appearance as if somebody tried to burn it.

What happened to Betty Necessary on February 1970 was a shock to the community of East Tennessee and the police wanted to give the community and Betty's family a sense of reassurance that the bastard that killed a child in their community was behind bars and would never do something like this again. If they tried Fred and convicted him for the murder of Betty Necessary, then he would get the death sentence or at least be behind bars for life and that is all the community wanted.

An Angel is Buried

Anybody that has ever had a loved one missing will tell you that until a body is found there is always hope. When the empty shell that housed our personality and our spirit is found hope will end and a bitter form of grief and resolution will begin. It is often said that at this point you heal, but for anybody that has ever lost a child it is unnatural part of your life. In the natural flow of life, a parent is supposed to die before their children; even when a child is sick, you know they will get better because that is just the way it is supposed to be.

The hope their child Betty would grow up to be a strong adult held out for Walter and Dorothy Necessary until they viewed the body of their little angel at Carter's Chapel. She seemed to have lain down and fallen asleep in the small coffin which would hold her body forever. The pink dress gave her back a youthful innocence and covered the indignities she suffered before death. Looking upon her was just like looking at the face of an angel and even in death, it was easy to see that had Betty lived would be a beautiful woman.

Neither Fred Bowen nor anybody else could ever hurt Betty again because God had her now. He sent his angels down to bring her back to Heaven so her broken body could be mended back good as new. The once beautiful voice silenced would sing again; she was restored to the dancing, happy child that filled so many hearts with sunshine. She would never know pain again; never know hunger, thirst or what humiliation was like. She would be surrounded by only love and happiness. Memories that were unpleasant would be gone and she was filled with only a wonderful light and the opportunity to be whole again.

Local newspapers reported that over 3,000 mourners paid their last respects to Betty and her family functioned as any family would, they knew they had to go on because they had other children that needed them. Betty didn't need them anymore like she did here on earth and the only thing that Betty needed now was justice. Family, friends, schoolmates, teachers and even those that didn't know Betty when she was alive, filed past her coffin in disbelief of what had happened to her. Some of her friends could not bear to go up to her coffin because the reality of what happened was too much for them so they stood back and watched, cried and tried the best they could to cope with being forced into an adult situation before they should have.

Betty's funeral was held at Hall Street Holiness Church and she was buried at East Lawn Memorial Park with a small but most befitting headstone with her favorite Bible verse Psalm 23:1 inscribed.

Carter's Chapel was the funeral home in charge of preparation of her body and they would take no money for their services, it was their contribution to her family.

The day that Betty was buried was a solemn day, and even the birds that had once been so jealous of Betty's voice were quiet. A sense of dread and disbelief fell on everyone because this was the second time Betty had been buried. The first time was a makeshift grave where she had been left by her killers, but this time they were placing her in her final resting place by everybody that loved her. Family members vowed before they left that whoever was responsible for this heinous crime would be brought to justice.

There was no way that whoever was responsible would get by without paying for it.

The Trial

Most people think that a trial is exactly what they see on television shows, but in real life they only share a slight resemblance. A real trial takes time, so evidence can be gathered and to get statements from witnesses. While in the courtroom the judge, audience and family will listen to testimony being presented and see evidence presented. For the family and friends of Betty it couldn't have been easy to listen to the last moments of her life.

This trial is one that everybody could tell would change the views of residents in Kingsport and in particular Bloomingdale. Even when the trial was over the changes would take hold and nobody would ever forget what had happened. Parents were watching their children closely and paying more attention to where they went and who they were with.

The money that Freddie was always flashing around must have run out being used to purchase cigarettes, guns or lost gambling because Judge John Byers appointed Shelburne Ferguson and Burkett McInturff as attorneys to represent Fred Bowen since he could not afford an attorney on his own.

Initially Mr. McInturff wanted the trial moved to Hawkins County due to excitement over two crime magazines, "Inside Detective" June 1970 issue and "Official Detective" July 1970 issue. Both magazines had widely been circulated and sold in Sullivan County so much that Fred's attorneys felt he could not receive a fair and constitutional trial. The motion for a change of venue was overruled and the trial continued in Kingsport.

One interesting aspect mentioned in the magazines was the unsolved murders of two young girls, Kathy Jones in Nashville and Glenda Sirmans in Knoxville which was also the same murders mentioned in the local newspapers; both of these murders occurred November 1969. Other agencies wanted to question Fred Bowen regarding the unsolved murders, however, this was never granted due to the possibility it may compromise the Betty Necessary case. Could he have committed these crimes? Sure, he was not employed and known to travel and trade guns, knives and jewelry. In 1970, the way the police investigated crimes was different because they were limited in ways to investigate, gather evidence and even viewed things different than what we do now. It was more important for the police to make the public feel safer again than to discover all the details to the crime or to even make sure anybody that was involved was prosecuted. Whether or not that Bowen committed these crimes is something that we will never know because this was never pursued as it should have been.

It was announced on March 5th, 1970 that the trial for Fred J. Bowen was set for June 1, 1970; however a motion for continuance was heard on May 15, 1970 and the trial was postponed until July 20th, 1970.

Evidence was carefully collected and over 150 pieces of evidence were gathered in the case. Residents of Kingsley Avenue were questioned and statements taken about the last time they have seen Betty and if they knew Fred Bowen. Police did not want to leave any stone unturned, no matter what.

Investigators even searched a large trash pile not far from the Laforce home since Fred and his father in law test fired rounds from a gun believed to have been used to kill Betty into the trash pile. When the bullets were recovered in the trash pile it was a significant boost to the case.

Interviews and statements were taken to check out Freddie's complex character since if he liked you he would give you the shirt off his back or if he hated you he would harass the hell out of you. Statements were taken prior to the court date being set, which helped establish a foundation for the trial. One being the bullets for the gun and the other being his being on Kingsley Avenue not long before Betty's murder. When the police interviewed Kingsley Avenue residents one of them told the police he had known Fred Bowen about 5 or 6 years. Fred used to park his old station wagon in front of his house and sleep in it when he had no place to stay. The last time he had seen Fred was on Sunday, February 22, 1970 around 7:30 or 8:00 in the morning driving his blue Pontiac car down from the direction of the Necessary home. He was sure it was Freddie Bowen because he stopped his car and visited with him before he drove down Kingsley Avenue. Why was Fred on Kingsley Avenue? That was never explained.

If you haven't gathered by now Freddie Bowen was not the sharpest pencil in the box and didn't understand a great deal about the English language. His lack of education was even more obvious when he was on the stand being questioned.

Fred did a great job of keeping his head down during most of the trial and his wife Sandra sat behind him. The family of Betty Necessary had to sit at least 6 rows behind Freddie while in court.

Edith Ketron, one of the witnesses who lived on Chadwell Road was called to testify and was very pregnant at the time of the trial. Her baby was due at any time and because of her condition she was put on the stand soon after the trial started and was one of the first to testify.

Mrs. Ketron testified that Fred was an acquaintance of her husband and had been in their home on several occasions. Fred approached her car on Friday, February 27th when she was returning home from taking some neighborhood children home after school. Fred wanted to know if her husband had any guns, Mrs. Ketron confirmed he did. Fred wanted to borrow a gun from her husband with shells, but he offered no reason for needing the gun and she didn't ask. If Fred had already killed Betty on Thursday the 26th then why was he trying to borrow a gun on the 27th? What was the gun going to be used for?

Mrs. Ketron testified she saw Fred later on that same day when he went up by their house in a car traveling slowly. She was in the kitchen by the window and noticed that he pulled almost to the top of the hill and then backed up and got out of the car. The vehicle he was in was blue with a dark top and she had seen him driving it before. Fred parked on the right side of the road, walked across the road toward Chadwell Pond then he stepped down and threw something toward the pond. She couldn't tell what it was other than it appeared to be white in color. Fred was wearing an orange shirt and the time was around 5:00 pm which was about 2 ½ hours after she spoke with Fred regarding the guns. Although there is a fence between the road and the pond she could see the person and testified it was Fred Bowen.

John Bishop who is a Criminal Investigator for the Sullivan County Sheriff's Department confirmed that he had a conversation with Mrs. Eva Ketron on March 4, 1970 and after the conversation went to the Kingsport Lifesaving Crew where he obtained a boat and the assistance of two crew members. In addition, he got a forty pound magnet and set of drag hooks normally used to drag for a human body. They went back to Chadwell Pond and put the boat in the water and dragged the pond by moving forwards and backwards across the pond using both the drag hooks and also the large magnet. After about 15 minutes, Mr. Lawrence Winegar and John Bishop hooked a slightly rusted .25 caliber automatic with one of the drag hooks. When the gun was found the handles was still on the gun and it was muddy, but still had the majority of bluing on it. Photos were made of the gun when it was taken out of the pond and taken to the Sheriff's Department where they were booked into evidence.

Verlon Ketron was the owner of a small local store not far from Chadwell Road and familiar with both Fred Bowen and Phillip Laforce. Mr. Ketron gave a statement to the police that Fred and Phillip came into his store on February 26, 1970 at about 11:00 am to purchase cigarettes and also wanted to purchase .25 caliber bullets. Bowen purchased about $29.00 worth of cigarettes and wanted to purchase bullets, but Mr. Ketron had none of the bullets he needed. Fred was big on productions and wanted Mr. Ketron to know that he had a lot of money so he pulled out a wad of cash and paid for his cigarettes making sure the store owner seen the money he had.

Mr. Ketron recalled the last time he seen Fred prior to his visit on February 26th was on November 27, 1969 when Fred bought two boxes of .22 caliber bullets. He also pointed out that when Fred came in he almost always brought Phillip with him.

One of the first witnesses for the State was Special Agent James Keesling who worked for the TBI and later on becoming the Chief of Police for Kingsport City. He was asked to describe the condition of the body of Betty Jean Necessary when it was discovered. He explained the body of Betty Necessary was found in the Bloomingdale section of Kingsport, Tennessee where she had been partially buried in a cave after being shot four (4) times in the back and once in the stomach after being viciously raped. A laceration was on her head and several tears and rips to the vagina and the surrounding area He was questioned about the damage done to the vagina and whether or not that another object could have caused the damage; he advised he didn't know what caused the damage to the vagina. He explained there was a tear in front and extended to the inside of the vagina and was visible from the outside of the body. There was blood in front of the vagina, which went all the way back into the rectum. When the body was found the wounds were not bleeding, the blood was dried, but might have leaked some when the body was removed from the location of the cave.

Agent Keesling was asked to describe the gags used on the victim and he told the jury besides an inner gag wadded up like a fist and placed deeply in her mouth there was also three outer gags that were looped one over the top of the other and knotted behind the victim's neck so tightly that one of the gags was pulled down and cut into the gums of the victim. When the gag wadded up in her mouth was removed it had blood and saliva on it. Agent Keesling also testified the hands or the victim were tied behind her back with three pieces of binding.

Special Agent Keesling explained to the Court that after completing the work at the hospital where the body of Betty Jean

Necessary had been taken; he interviewed several people including Sandra Bowen and Phillip Laforce. Phillip was taken to the police department for questioning and after Phil was interviewed, Fred Bowen was brought to the Safety Building at around 8:20 pm on February 28, 1970 arrested after his rights were read to him then he was charged with first degree murder.

Fred told the police he would talk to them, but refused to sign a waiver.

According to Agent Keesling hair samples were taken from Fred for comparison which comprised head, chest, midsection and pubic hairs. Pubic hairs were pulled out by Mr. Bowen and given to Agent Keesling who placed them in an envelope for analysis.

Agent Keesling explained to the Court that during questioning Fred answered the questions sensibly; however he evaded some questions.

After he was questioned Fred was told that he was charged with the murder of Betty Jean Necessary.

Fred J. Bowen was called to the stand, as he approached glaring eyes full of hatred looked at him.

Fred was questioned about his employment and he testified before he and Sandra came to Kingsport in February 1970 he was not working at a regular job and hadn't been for about three months. His last regular job was at Standard Brands making about $87.00 a week, but didn't go into why he was no longer employed there. Since he left Standard Brands, he made his living by trading, and selling various antiques, guns, jewelry and things of that nature. Fred was asked about his ability to sign his name and he confirmed that he could sign his name but couldn't read nor write; although he could read small words he recognized from memory.

Fred was questioned about the extent of his education and he told the court he attended Kingsley Elementary School up to the sixth grade and then quit.

Fred was interviewed by his attorney Mr. McInturff and since Fred's intelligence was limited he used terms out of context his lack of intelligence and formal education was painfully obvious. The only reason that his attorney could have had for letting him take the stand was to demonstrate that Fred did not have enough sense to perpetrate this crime.

70

Most people know what size of clothing they wear, even young children will know their clothes size, but when asked, Fred was not sure what size clothing and boots he wore. His method of purchasing shirts and clothing was to make a guess on whether the items would fit him at the department store, purchase them and if they fit he wore them and if they didn't he discarded them.

Fred testified that he spent the night of Wednesday, February 25th with his half-brother, Andrew Bowen. After he woke up, he went downstairs to Bloomingdale Drive-In and ate breakfast and then he drove to the Laforce house on Chadwell Road where his wife Sandra was staying. On Thursday he worked on his car and washed it and then he shot arrows with a bow in a field in front of Carl Laforce's house, the time was midday.

Fred drove back over to Bloomingdale Drive-In and after he ate lunch he drove to a bank downtown Kingsport and did business then to see a jeweler also in downtown Kingsport and finally returned to the Bloomingdale Drive-In for a cup of coffee at about 4:30 pm.

Fred was questioned about the diamonds he brought with him when he came to Tennessee from Indiana and he testified that when he left Indiana, he had about $12,000 worth of diamonds and on Thursday he had about $7000 worth of diamonds left- while he had been in Tennessee he had either sold or traded $5000 worth of diamonds not bad for a 6th grade drop out that couldn't keep a job for over 6 months.

Fred's physical condition on the night of his arrest was also questioned and it was revealed that he was taken to Holston Valley Hospital by his in-laws on Saturday February 28th due to flu like conditions and also running a fever. The doctor told him he almost had pneumonia. He was given a prescription for medication, but couldn't recall the name of the medication only that he was instructed not to drive while taking it. He was also given a prescription for cough medicine which he had filled at the drug store in Bloomingdale.

Fred testified that he was picked up on Saturday at Sandra's grandmother's house by the police and taken in for questioning. Fred could identify Agent Keesling, somebody named Bill and

John Bishop. There was another person present, but he didn't know his name and only described him as a short man.

Fred was questioned more about the night of his arrest and confirmed that Phillip Laforce had visited him that night, but he wouldn't say what their conversation comprised, he even commented about not understanding Phillip and what he was saying. The court pointed out that his comment made little sense since he had known Phil for several years, why suddenly could he not understand him?

During questioning Fred was also asked questions that normal people will know such as the year he was born, where he was born, the name of his father and level of education- this was done to establish the intelligence level he had. Fred knew the year he was born and explained that he was sure he was born in Virginia; however, he told the courtroom he did not know the name of his father.

Fred testified that he had been convicted of burglary and one more charge of petit larceny. Fred was asked about whether that he knew Betty Jean Necessary and he testified that he did not know her nor did he kill her.

Items taken into evidence were shown to Fred and he denied owning the boots and a brown sweater, but he confirmed in court, he had packed brown sweaters for his trip while in Kingsport. Fred testified that he owned a .25 caliber pistol similar to the gun entered in evidence found in Chadwell Pond, but the gun in evidence was not his gun. Fred was questioned about prior injuries to his head and he confirmed he had either three or four injuries and one blackout spell he could recall. The first injury occurred when he was younger and had a bicycle wreck and was knocked unconscious from the injury. The other ones occurred when he was involved in an auto accident and bumped his head on the roof of the car. He also had a head injury in Indianapolis while employed in the Fall of 1969 when he fell about 22 steps where he former worked at and injured his head.

Fred was asked about beating up something at the Laforce house and his response was that it was a piece of metal from his tape recorder and denied it was any part of a gun. He also denied throwing anything into Chadwell Pond.

Fred confirmed that he purchased a .25 caliber pistol while in Tennessee which was common for him to do since he bought and traded guns often, but he said that he sold the gun to a guy down at the truck stop for $45.00 on Wednesday night after 12:00. Unfortunately, he did not recall the name of the person he sold the gun to and he had not seen him since.

Fred was asked about whether he had done any hunting or shooting while he had been in Tennessee in the woods near the Laforce house and confirmed he had. He indicated that on Monday morning and Tuesday evening and on Thursday in particular on Thursday he was up above the Laforce house in the trash pile shooting a .22 pistol, a Derringer and his bow and arrow.

Fred told the court when he came to Tennessee he slept in his clothes at night because it was cold in both the Dunn and Laforce houses so he always slept in his clothing to stay warm. He also confirmed to the court, he was not wearing a T-shirt or boots on February 26th; instead of boots he was wearing slippers.

75

Fred had made an appointment with a jeweler in downtown Kingsport for Thursday February 26th at 3:30 pm and he kept the appointment. He got back from downtown Kingsport about 4:30 pm and went directly to the Bloomingdale Drive-In. He had a cup of coffee and told Andrew he had a deal on diamonds he was trying to sell. Fred told the court he stayed there about 30 minutes at the Drive-In and then went back to the Laforce house where he shot the bow/arrow and gun in the woods behind the house. When he was finished, he took the weapons back to his car put the gun in the glove compartment and put the bow& arrow in his vehicle. He went back over to his brother's grill and sat in his car out front, he was feeling sick and was trying to make up his mind whether that he wanted to go to the doctor. He wasn't there about 5 or 10 minutes when Marvin Bowen came out of the restaurant- it was about 5:10 pm or 5:15 pm and told him he better take the car home so he left and went to Rose Dunn's house. While parked in the driveway at the Dunn residence, he blew his horn and in a few minutes Phillip Laforce came outside to see what he wanted and he told Phil to get in the car. They went to the liquor store located down on the Super Highway and he gave Phil some money for two fifths of liquor. While Phil was in the liquor store getting the liquor Fred stayed outside and helped a man boost his car off and get the running.

After Phil came out and got in the car the two men went back to the Bloomingdale Drive-In. He hadn't been there long when Andrew discovered that he had been drinking so he took the keys to his car away because he felt like Freddie was too intoxicated to drive safely. Fred left his car at the restaurant and walked back home with Phil to Rosie Dunn's house. The walk wasn't that far for a young man like Freddie and was only about two miles away. While Fred and Phil walked home they met up with Sandra, who was in the car with a friend.

Fred was asked to recall the argument between him and his wife on February 28th and in particular something regarding a red headed girl. Mr. McInturff asked him what he said about the red headed girl that apparently had caused arguments between the two. Fred replied that he said that he would like to kill that red headed bitch. Asked what the girl had done to him his response was that she had told a lot of lies about him and his wife before they got married. Fred explained the altercation with Sandra occurred because she found out that he had been drinking. Sandra was mad at Fred and swung her pocketbook hitting him over the eye which caused a scratch. Fred pointed out that he did not hit her back and had never hit her before either. While on the stand he also denied telling Sandra and Phil he had killed somebody. He was asked again if he bound, gagged, raped and killed the Necessary girl to which Fred replied "no".

When Fred reached his destination that night he and Phil went directly to Rose Dunn's house and stayed there all night. He left out the next day about 11:00 am and went back down the road and told the neighbor where he caused a disturbance he was sorry for disturbing them the night before and then he went to the Bloomingdale Drive-In where his car was still parked.

When General Kirkpatrick cross-examined Fred he asked about him working in the diamond business; Fred told General Kirkpatrick he did a little bit of everything. He indicated that he was doing well in the diamond business. Fred was questioned about how long it had been since he worked at a regular job and he answered it was about seven or eight months. While he was unemployed, he had accumulated about $12,000 worth of diamonds. He was asked if he had been dealing in diamonds on a part time basis and how he had accumulated $12,000 worth of diamonds- what had he done with all these diamonds. While in Tennessee he sold diamonds to many people but could not remember the names of the people. Some paid him in cash and some traded other items. He had approximately $7000 worth of diamonds left on the 26th of February which meant that he had sold and/or traded $5000 worth of diamonds. Part of the $5000 was in money and part of it was traded items such as rings. Since he kept no record of what he had sold and what had been traded he didn't know how much cash he had made.

Fred told the court that one person he remembered selling items to be in downtown Kingsport on a corner, next to a little restaurant; he knew that at one time this jeweler had his shop up over Todd and Dossett Law Office then he then moved his shop downstairs. General Kirkpatrick asked Fred had the jeweler moved while he was in Kingsport on his visit and he answered that the jeweler had not moved while he was in for the visit he just knew that at one time the jeweler was in the upstairs location. The defendant could not tell how much business he had conducted with the jeweler, but he told the court the first time he made a sale with the jeweler was on Tuesday the 24th of February and he sold him diamonds for cash in about $40.00. Fred went back on Wednesday and traded around lunch time and returned that evening to discuss trading more with the jeweler.

Fred wasn't sure whether it was Wednesday or Thursday, but he knew one of the days he took Donnie Bowen with him to the jeweler because there was a ring in the jeweler's case that Donnie wanted. Fred sold two large size diamonds and the jeweler also took diamonds out of the mountings for him. Some diamonds that Fred brought in was swapped out for a ring in the jewelry case with a price on it of $249.95 and he also gave Fred $15.00 or $20.00 to boot.

General Kirkpatrick asked Fred what he and Donnie had discussed between the two when he went with Fred to the jeweler and Fred wouldn't admit to a discussion with Donnie. He was asked what relation that Donnie was to him, he was not sure. He told General Kirkpatrick that Donnie was Andrew's son and Andrew was his half-brother. General Kirkpatrick thought Fred's answer was strange and although he continued trying to find out from Fred the relationship with Donnie Bowen he was never successful in finding out more.

Fred testified that after he got back from the jeweler's store he went to the Bloomingdale Drive-In, which was around 5:00 pm and drank a cup of coffee and stayed from 5-15 minutes. After he left, he went back over to pick up Phil Laforce after which both proceeded to the liquor store, then back to Bloomingdale Drive-In which was around 7:00 to 8:00pm. Fred told the court he knew it was about that time because he got a phone call from his brother in Indianapolis while he was there.

Fred was asked if he knew Mrs. Ketron that lives up next to the pond and he testified that he knew both her and her husband and he met them when he went with his wife Sandra. He was asked again about what time he got to the Dunn residence to pick up Phil and

81

he testified that it was about 5:30 when he got there. He went over to the fence row, which was around 75 to 100 feet above the house. He was asked if it could have been as far as 200 feet and he said no.

Fred admitted in court he did not go see his wife and her family when he returned from his various trips while in Kingsport because they were always arguing and he wanted to avoid this. He deliberately avoided the Laforce house altogether, except to park his car.

Fred mentioned that during the week of the 26th he was sick with the flu, almost pneumonia, burning up with fever to the point of where he had to go to the hospital. However, it is strange that the sickness didn't slow him down. He still could shoot the gun and bows & arrows, even go the jeweler trade diamonds and several trips to the Bloomingdale Drive-In.

During the court case often Fred was asked about the sweater size he wore and was presented a sweater in evidence which was a size large; however, it barely fit him- and he denied the sweater was his even though it was found in a suitcase where he had been staying at Rose Dunn's house. Fred was asked where his boots were since he maintained he wore slippers that day and he advised they were in the back of his car where he had put them on Wednesday; they had to be there because he was the only one with a key to his car. General Kirkpatrick implied during his examination that Fred knew where the cave was located because he had lived in that area all of his life and had been through the woods and knew them well. Fred told the court he knew there was a lot of "holes" in the area with tin cans in them, but he did not know where that cave was located. He said that he had never been to that cave before and although he had lived in that area most of his life and had walked through the woods hundreds of times was not looking for caves he was hunting for squirrels.

General Kirkpatrick also mentioned the pieces of T-shirt used as a gag come from the T-shirt right off of Fred's back and that is the reason all fibers in Fred's clothing was on the gag material. When asked if he had been in the Laforce home, he said that he had been home some of that day and that he also had gone to the bank in the afternoon after lunch. General Kirkpatrick told him he had been home that day at 2:00 and had gone to the cave and he had seen the Necessary girl before and he planned it right there. During this period of time Fred denied what General Kirkpatrick was saying and again told the court he was at the Bloomingdale Drive-In at 2:00 and not at home. General Kirkpatrick told him he had a .25 caliber gun and that he decided to get the little girl so he removed his shirt and got it ready to use as a gag. General Kirkpatrick's hypothesis couldn't have been far off when he stated in court that when the little child came walking up the road by herself he knew he had the opportunity he needed. When she walked down those woods there he was right behind her with a pistol in her back and she got scared and dropped or threw her books and ran and that is when he hit her in the head with the pistol and put a gash in her head. Then he marched her down to that area where her clothes were found where he bound and gagged her, when she was at his mercy he raped her brutally on the spot. For whatever reason, only known to him, Fred wrapped her coat around her and walked her to the cave. While she was still bleeding, hurting and gagged/bound she was shot in the front abdominal region. This small girl still a child went to her knees with her hands still bound behind her back Fred shot Betty four more times in her back and it gets worse because she was buried while she was still alive. During this long accusation Fred continued to deny that he did anything and denied that he hurt her- everything was all denials.

Bud Adams, who is the owner/operator for Bloomingdale Phillips 66 Service Station was called to testify as witness for the State. According to Mr. Adams he had known Fred about 2 years and originally met him when he opened up the service station. Fred would work for him occasionally when he needed money. To the best of his memory, he thought he had seen Fred on Tuesday before Betty's murder when Fred came in for an oil change. During this visit Fred had two guns with him; one of them was a small gun broke up from the bottom and the other was an automatic with pearl handles and was possibly a .25 automatic. Fred wanted to sell the gun with pearl handles for $50.00 and Mr. Adams told Fred he wasn't interested so Fred put the guns up. When cross examined, Mr. Adams testified that sometimes Fred had worked for him when he came in from Indiana and didn't have any money for repairs to be done to his car. He put Fred to work cleaning the garden, and the extra lot at his home, then Fred paid him for the repairs to his car.

Mr. Adams told the court he had two teenage daughters and when Fred worked for him his daughters would be around. He had never been told by his girls of any problems with Fred and as far as he knew, he had acted respectful around them.

Mr. Adams told the court he knew Phillip Laforce from the gas station as well and had to run him off when Phillip brought in some sex magazines and tried to show them to him and his workers.

Ina Begley lived on Kingsley Avenue and was a neighbor to the Necessary's. She had known Betty Jean Necessary for the past few years. Mrs. Begley told the court the road that went from her house to Betty's house was thickly wooded on one side and had several trees on the other. Betty lived at the top of the hill and there was only one house between her house and the Necessary house. Recalling February 26th she testified that she was home and had seen Betty Necessary on that day at 3:40 pm. The reason she remembered the time was that she thought her children should have been home from school and she was a little uneasy why they weren't home yet. She opened the front door to give her a better view and that is when she seen Betty coming from the Hickman house next door and cut across the yard while keeping straight on the road. The last time she has seen Betty was at 3:42 pm when Betty was on the upper side of the garden near the woods.

Wanda Hickman was a friend of Betty Necessary and she walked to school with her every day. It had to be very stressful for the young eighth grader to testify, but she bravely told the court she and her sister Joyce were friends with Betty. Wanda and her family live next door to Ina Begley and her home was the last stop that Betty made before disappearing on February 26th. Betty only stopped for about 3-4 minutes to see the new baby just brought home from the hospital. She confirmed the last time she has seen Betty Necessary was on February 26th when was walking toward her home, going up the hill. She saw nobody else walking with her and saw no cars or traffic on Kingsley Road during the time Betty was walking.

87

John Bishop is a Criminal Investigator for the Sullivan County Sheriff's Department. Mr. Bishop was present during the discovery of Betty's body and also helped search the home of Rose Dunn and found several items belonging to Fred Bowen introduced as evidence.

The day after the search of the Dunn property, John Bishop went to the residence of Carl Laforce and after having a conversation with Mr. Laforce searched the Laforce property which yielded three bullet shell casings about 30 feet down a hill from a garbage pile toward the Laforce house.

According to testimony from Mr. Bishop, Carl Laforce came to Blountville later on that day and turned over a .32 caliber pistol to him and after speaking again with Mr. Laforce went back to Chadwell Road to the residence of Rose Dunn to search a culvert well grown over with weeds & grass. A tile in the culvert was about 12 inches in diameter and was on the public road. Although the property had been thoroughly searched before, a pair of boots was about 30 feet to the right side of the Dunn house. Nobody is sure whether boots were not there at the time of the initial searches and simply overlooked which is possible, however unlikely. The only other possible option was the boots were planted after the searches had taken place.

Johnny A. Robertson is an investigator with the Sullivan County Sheriff's Department and he confirmed that he was present when the body of Betty Necessary was discovered. He also told the court he had been at the Dunn residence three times between February 28th and March 4th.

Mr. Robertson was present in the morgue at the Holston Valley Community Hospital when Dr. Harrison examined the body of Betty Necessary. During the examination Dr. Harrison found three pubic hairs on the body and also probed the body for the bullets, four bullets were located and removed. Officer Robertson confirmed that he and Officer Keesling packaged items that comprised clothing type evidence, including: trousers, two T-shirt strips, both were described as used as outer gags, a T-shirt strip described as an inner gag, another strip of cloth, described as a wrist binding, brassiere, a blouse, one shoe, a pair of boots, brown sweater, and a coat. Evidence was also packaged that comprised:

two soil samples from the cave, hair, a .25 caliber slug, and some pieces of plastic bits or splinters. All items were packaged and driven by J.C. Fletcher in a Sullivan County Sheriff's car to Washington, D.C., and turned over to Agent Smith and Agent Scholberg.

Lucille Laforce was called to testify and told the court she was the mother in law of Fred Bowen; her daughter Sandra is married to him. Lucille is married to Carl Laforce and they have three children, Phillip is 21; Sandra is 20 and Timmy is 10. According to Mrs. Laforce, Sandra and Fred had been living in Indianapolis, Indiana for several months and they came in to visit back in February 1970.

On Thursday the 26th, Mrs. Laforce was at home with Timmy, who was sick with the flu and Sandra was also there with them. Fred came home about 2:00 pm or possibly 2:05 pm, she knew the time because there was a soap opera on that she watches every day and is well acquainted with the time it comes on. She recalled that Fred was talking low to Sandra and he took a roll of pink paper towels sitting on top of the dryer, tore several sheets off and went out the door toward the direction of the outdoor toilet on top of the hill. When Fred left the house, Sandra stayed there with her mother and Timmy. Mrs. Laforce saw Fred again later on in the afternoon when she was pouring out waste water at about 4:30 pm and he was coming out thru the woods behind their home but not from the direction of their outdoor toilet. Mrs. Laforce went back into the house to fix supper and looked through the door and noticed Fred was standing under a big tree, staring at the ground like he was thinking deeply about something. She continued preparing supper and her attention was called back out to Fred again when she heard a pecking noise and looked out the window to see Fred was holding something white in Fred's hands. He was standing at the pile of cinder block in their yard. Unfortunately, she could not tell what Fred was holding only it was something white. Shortly after the noise stopped and she heard a car door slam and noticed Fred had left.

Mrs. Laforce didn't see Fred again until late that evening at about 8:00 pm or 8:30 pm when he was at Rose Dunn's house. Their son Phillip came by and told Mr. and Mrs. Laforce he and Fred would stay all night at the Dunn home. Mr. Laforce asked his wife to go over to the Dunn residence and see what was wrong. The comment that Mr. Laforce made to his wife made no sense since Fred and Phil had been staying with Ms. Dunn while they had been in Kingsport. Phillip Laforce had been staying with her all of his life. Mrs. Laforce was questioned about the clothing that Fred was wearing on February 26th, and she testified that Fred was wearing brown-gold type pants and a brown sweater with black slip on style boots. She was not sure of what type of boot they were, only remembered them being slip on type.

Mrs. Laforce mentioned nothing to her husband Carl about the events that day or the strange pecking noise she heard coming from the cinder block pile. Nothing was mentioned about the strange actions of Fred until Saturday the 28th when she went out with her husband to the cinder block pile and discovered white pieces of an unidentified hard material. Mr. Laforce picked up the material and placed them in his pocket for the time being and later on giving them to the police.

Fred had been sick and on Saturday, February 28th, Fred asked the Laforce's to take him to the hospital to get a shot because he thought he was getting the flu. They took him to the hospital and stayed in the parking lot while Fred went into the hospital. Fred came out a little later on and told the Laforce's he seen the doctor and could not get the shot because he had the flu too long. He was given a prescription and the Laforce's drove him to the drug store in Bloomingdale where he had the prescription filled after they were done at the drug store the Laforce's and Fred went to the grocery store and then home.

Later on that day Fred was arrested at the Laforce home and Mrs. Laforce didn't see Fred again until she took him a birthday cake to the jail the Sunday before his birthday which was April 23rd. She read him the name on the birthday cake and also read the birthday card to him. Mrs. Laforce was at the jail with her husband and Andrew Bowen but only spoke with Fred briefly so it would give him time to visit his brother. Fred called her to the window and told her the thing she seen him breaking up at the cinder block pile was a piece off his tape recorder. While Fred probably wanted a response from her, she just walked away.

Mrs. Laforce was cross examined by Mr. McInturff and asked about any blood being on his clothing and she responded that she didn't noticed any blood on his pants or shirt. She was asked if she knew anything about red clay mud in the area where they lived and she responded there was a field would get muddy when it rained but didn't think that it was red clay.

Mrs. Laforce was questioned about her son Phillip's whereabouts and she testified that on February 26th she saw Phillip about 4:00pm when he came in and told her he had been with Johnny Riley helping him work on his car. He left shortly after telling his mother where he had been and walked over to his grandmother's house. She saw Phillip later that night at about 8:30pm when Phillip told his mother he and Fred would spend the night at Rose Dunn's house.

Mrs. Laforce testified that Phillip was arrested and taken to the police department on Saturday, while she and her husband were away with Fred at the hospital. While Phillip was still in custody the police showed up and arrested Fred Bowen. Phillip was released on Saturday night (Feb. 28th) shortly after Fred's arrest. Sandra Louise Laforce Bowen, the wife of Fred Bowen was a mousey nervous person, she was questioned by General Kirkpatrick. Sandra testified that when they drove back to Kingsport from Indiana in February 1970, the occupants in the car were her brother Phillip, Fred, Sandra and Fred's aunt; Sandra oddly could not recall her name. Phillip had been living with them in Indiana for about three weeks and they came to Kingsport for a visit since Sandra had vacation time from work.

Sandra testified that she worked at Standard Brands Corporation and Fred was unemployed, however, he had been trading guns, antiques and also gambled which he was very good at according to Sandra. While visiting in Kingsport Sandra had been staying with her parents except for one night spent at Andrew Bowen's house. Sandra was asked about what she remembered on February 26th and she responded that she could only vaguely remember the day. She spent the night at her parent's house while Fred stayed at her grandmother's house. She saw Fred the first time on Thursday at about 8:30-9:00 in the morning when he came over for breakfast and Fred stayed at the Laforce home until Andrew opened up his grill and then he left she assumed to go to the brother's grill. Fred came back at around 11:00 that morning and picked up Sandra and both of them went to Andrew's grill for about an hour. On their way home, they stopped at her grandmother's house and then she returned to her parent's home.

Sandra continued to tell the court that Phillip and Fred had been talking on Thursday and decided they would drive to Virginia and get cigarettes. Virginia is located less than two miles from Chadwell Road where the Laforce home was located. You can purchase cigarettes in Virginia since the cigarettes and taxes are cheaper. Fred came back to the Laforce home at about 2:00pm alone and stayed there until shortly after 2:00pm when he told his wife he was going up on the hill to the outdoor toilet. As far as Sandra knew Fred was alone when he went up the hill, she did not watch him as he left to see in what direction he was going. Sandra didn't see Fred again until 4:30pm when she went to get the paper out of the paper box. She could establish the time because she was watching a show on television that coincided with the time. Sandra heard the paper woman stop and went out to get the paper; she noticed Fred was standing in the yard just staring.

Sandra identified in court the brown sweater that Fred was wearing on February 26th and the cowboy boots he had on. She told the courtroom that Fred packed his own bag before they left Indiana to come to Kingsport and she was not sure of what was in his suitcase.

Phillip Laforce was called as witness and testified that he had been living with his grandmother, Rose Dunn since birth. His mother and father, Lucille and Carl Laforce lived next to his grandmother, which made it easy for him to visit with both households and help out as much as possible. Phillip was of the same caliber as Fred and most people in the community knew he wasn't very intelligent. He had no regular job and only worked some odd part time jobs which gave him the opportunity to stay with Sandra and Fred in Indiana for a few weeks. Phillip had to come back home from Indiana mainly because Mrs. Dunn could not help care for herself and his job was to carry coal and water to her house. Phillip had been staying with Sandra and Fred since early February in Indiana and while he was gone his grandmother was staying elsewhere with a relative.

When he returned with Sandra and Fred to Kingsport in February he resumed living with his grandmother again.

Phillip was questioned about being in trouble with the law before and he testified he had been sent to jail for one day and was fined when he had stolen pop bottles. Back in the 1960's and 1970's it was common for people to collect the empty glass containers that soda pop would come in to return them to a local retailer to collect the deposit paid by the original purchaser. You didn't get a great deal of money back, but you would get a few coins that would buy more soda pop or cigarettes in Phil's case. It was common for households to collect the glass bottles and return them on weekly shopping trips.

Phillip was asked where he spent the night before Betty Necessary disappeared and he testified that he had been at his grandmother's house. Phillip explained to the court, he has seen Fred on the Thursday that Betty Necessary disappeared about 11:00 am or

12:00 pm and wasn't sure, but thought Fred left earlier that morning to go to his brothers grill. He confirmed that he and Fred went to Mr. Ketron's store which is across the state line in Virginia to get cigarettes and afterwards went to Andrew's grill about lunch time. Fred talked a while at the grill, then played pinball and finally left with a man that Phillip recognized as working at the bank located across the street from the grill. According to Phillip, Fred didn't stay long with the man from the bank and came back into the grill and seemed in good spirits since he was laughing and played pinball again.

While at the grill, Phillip saw one of his friends, Johnny Riley, who asked Phillip to help him work on the carburetor in his car. Phillip agreed to help his friend and told Fred where he would be, and asked Fred to tell them at home he would be back later. Fred nodded his head and told him he would see him later. After Phillip and Johnny got through working on the car they stopped at the Gateway Market and purchased two quarts of beer which they drank on the way home. They ran into a group of friends and drove around the back roads to avoid being caught by the police while they drank the beer. Johnny Riley dropped Phillip off at the Laforce home at about 4:00 pm and Phillip told the court he wanted to get home before his father got home from work because if he found out that Phillip had been drinking he would have beat him. The worry was needless because when he arrived his dad was not home yet. Phillip was greeted by his mother, sister and brother; Fred was not home yet so he went to his grandmother's house and spoke briefly with his grandmother and then sat down on the couch after he took his boots off.

Phillip had not been on the couch long when he heard a car go up the road with the horn blowing and he went outside to see what was going on, it was Fred Bowen. Fred parked his car in the driveway and Phillip sat down with Fred in the car and the two talked and joked with one another about what they had been doing during the day after they had parted company. Fred told Phillip he had been "up there" pointing toward the woods and he had accidentally shot somebody. Phillip told the court that Fred told him he was shooting into some bushes when he heard somebody yell loudly. When Fred went to investigate, he discovered the person was dead; however Fred would not say who it was or the exact location of where the "accident" had occurred. When Phillip acted shocked and started asking questions Fred told Phillip he was only joking and to quit taking everything so seriously.

Fred asked Phillip to go with him to get liquor and assured him they would not be gone that long. Phillip testified that Fred had on a pair of yellow pants, a brown sweater and some boots. He had been wearing the same clothes for two or three days, so the clothing was dirty. They drove to the liquor store and Fred gave Phillip a $100.00 bill to purchase the liquor. Phillip purchased two fifths, one Old Grand Dad and the other was Rocking Chair. Fred drank some of the liquor, but Phillip drank no liquor explaining to the court that liquor makes him sick. When they left the liquor store they went to the Bloomingdale Grill; however, they didn't go inside as normal. Fred and Phillip stayed out in the car while Fred raced his motor and blew the horn, which went on for about two to three minutes until Andrew came out to talk to Fred. After a brief discussion Andrew determined that Fred had been drinking and asked for the keys to the car. Andrew told Fred he would not drive in that condition because he would either hurt himself or somebody else. Fred kept laughing and then finally gave the keys to Andrew. Andrew went back inside his grill and after a few moments came back out with his son Donnie and brought two glasses to get some of the liquor. After pouring liquor for each they put the bottles back behind the seat where they had been previously. Phillip and Fred stayed at the café for about an hour and then headed home by foot. On their way home Fred and Phillip ran into Sandra and she was with a girlfriend in a car. After they had a brief conversation with each other, Sandra and her friend went on to the laundry mat and Fred and Phillip walked again, Fred is staggering as he walked. Sandra had been gone for a only a few minutes when she came back and accused Fred of being drunk, which he denied and finally admitted he had only been drinking a little. Sandra was crying and Phillip didn't want to get into the middle of the fight so he went to the other side of the road. As the couple fussed, their voices grew louder and Phillip asked them to keep it down since he was afraid somebody would call the police. During the entire ruckus one of the neighbors turned on their outside porch light and

looked out of the window to see what the commotion was about.
Fred yelled at the neighbor to turn out the light or he would shoot it
out while exchanging angry words with one another. This
continued for a few moments and only stopped when the
neighbor's wife told her husband to get his gun and put it between
Fred's eyes.

Fred continued to swear as they walked and argued and Sandra
kept hitting him over the head with her pocketbook. Phillip could
finally get Sandra and Fred to quiet down so they could get home.
Phillip testified that he saw no blood on Fred that night and the
only thing he noticed out of the ordinary was Fred seemed a little
intoxicated. During the altercation and while Sandra was hitting
Fred he never tried to hit her back only warded off the blows. That
night Phillip, Sandra and Fred stayed at Rose Dunn's house and
Fred's car remained at the grill.

The next day Phillip testified that he has seen Donnie Bowen
driving Fred's car with Fred as the passenger. Marvin Bowen
which is Donnie's brother was in another car behind Donnie and
Fred. The purpose of this trip was to return Fred's vehicle back to

the Laforce house and avoid being caught by one of the numerous police officer's that were on patrol heavily that day. Phillip told the court that from Friday to Saturday evening he didn't leave the location of his parent's or his grandmother's home.

Mr. McInturff cross examined Phillip, who testified that he was also known by the nickname "Wildcat". When Mr. McInturff asked Phillip if he was called Wildcat because of his reputation of wild sexual deviations, Phillip denied this and said it wasn't true. He was asked about taking male magazines to the local filling stations and showing employees the pictures Phil responded there were magazines in his car and the employees found them when making repairs on his vehicle. Since that happened, he no longer took the magazines around in his car.

Phillip was asked about having sexual relations and he told the court he was unable since he fell on a big rock and somehow hurt himself. Phillip testified that he continued to have medical problems to the point when he urinated he had to hold onto something while urinating, not explaining the reason he had to do this. The story regarding the medical problems he described was never verified by a doctor or medical records.

Phillip testified that he was familiar with the road that led to the Necessary home, and knew where the cave was. He was also familiar with the old roadway that leads from Kingsley Road down through the ravine into the woods and the last time he was in the woods was last summer.

Phillip told the court that after he was taken downtown for questioning, he told the police about the conversation he had with Fred and the police kept telling him that if he didn't tell the truth he would be in prison for 15 years. While Phillip was on the stand he admitted that he knew that "everybody said he did it" but denied killing anyone.

Whether or not he assisted Fred with this crime in anyway was never questioned beyond this point and was never pursued as a possibility.

Carl Laforce was called as a witness; he is the father of Sandra, Phillip and Tim Laforce. Mr. Laforce testified that Fred asked him where he could get a small gun and he told Fred he knew somebody named Lloyd that sold guns and they went to see him. Lloyd wanted more than what Fred was willing to pay for a gun so they went to see Henry McMullen, who also sold guns and lived in the Vermont area of Bloomingdale. After going back and forth on the price of a gun, Fred and Henry finally decided on a price of $40.00 for a .25 automatic and Fred purchased shells from him. When they got back home Fred wanted to try the gun out so they went to a trash pile and both Mr. Laforce and Fred fired the gun several times at a target in the trash pile. Mr. Laforce described the gun that Fred purchased as small blue steel with a white handle and he wasn't for sure what Fred did with the gun after that day. A gun was presented to Mr. Laforce was asked if he recognized it. The gun was taken from Chadwell Pond and he told them it looked like the same size, but the bluing was removed from it.

Mr. Laforce was questioned about pieces of white chips he found in the cinder block pile and testified to the court his wife had told him later on Friday, February 27th about the noises coming from the pile of cinder block but it was too dark to see anything that night. He could look at the cinder block pile on Saturday morning and found small chips of white plastic, but did not pick them up and just left them where they were. It was later on after he heard about the Necessary murder he picked up the pieces of white plastic and put them in his shirt pocket. Later on when interviewed by the police he gave the pieces he had found to the police officer and also discussed with the police that a gun had been test fired into a garbage pile pointing out the area. Several of the police officers checked the garbage pile and found a copper bullet. Mr. Laforce told the court that Fred purchased a .38 Colt from him on Saturday morning and Mr. Laforce gave him 5 or 6 shells for the gun. He told the court he wasn't sure, but thought Fred either gave the gun to his brother Andrew or had left it on Andrew's grill.

On Saturday, February 28th, Mr. Laforce asked Fred about the.25 caliber gun he had purchased from Mr. McMullen when they were parked in front of the pharmacy waiting for his prescription to be filled.

Fred told his father in law, he sold the .25 caliber pistol at the truck stop for a truck driver on his way to New York for $50.00.

Mr. Laforce testified that he and his wife visited Fred in April while he was in jail for his birthday and they took him a cake. Fred told Mrs. Laforce during this visit the white plastic was not part of a gun, but was part of a tape recorder. While the Laforce's were visiting Fred, his brother Andrew was also visiting with him and Fred told Andrew he sold the .25 caliber gun to a boy for $45.00. Henry McMullen was called as a witness on behalf of the State and testified that he has lived for 30 years in the Vermont Section of Kingsport. Mr. McMullen is self employed as a well digger and he knew Carl Laforce; however, didn't know Fred Bowen until the night he came over to trade guns. Mr. McMullen was not for sure on the date, but he remembered it was about 4-5 days before Betty Necessary disappeared and it was late in the evening. Fred came with his father in law, Carl Laforce and they wanted to know if he had a .25 automatic they could look at for purchase. Fred had two guns with him, one was an Alvery Johnson and he wasn't sure about the other one. Mr. McMullen did not want to sell the .25 caliber gun and Fred kept on asking him until he priced the gun higher than what he thought Fred would pay; however Fred wanted the gun and purchased it. Besides selling him the gun he also sold him a box of .25 caliber copper jacket shells which is a bullet that flattens out after it is fired and does its damage from tearing and ripping.

Mr. McMullen had never fired the gun prior to his sale to Fred even though he owned the gun for two years. He was presented a gun to identify while in court and he admitted that he was not exactly sure, but it appeared to be the gun he sold to Fred, Frederick P. Smith, Jr., a Special Agent for the FBI was called as witness for the State. Agent Smith works in Washington, DC and examined the bullets and weapon used in connection with the murder of Betty Necessary. Mr. Smith testified that when a weapon is manufactured the barrel, firing pin and other surfaces have distinct marks left on it from the manufacturing process. The marks will change somewhat through the use of a weapon; however, will remain individually characteristic to that weapon. When a cartridge is fired, the marks on the surfaces of the weapon are transplanted on the bullet as it passes thru the barrel or is transplanted on the cartridge by the firing pin. When Agent Smith received the Galesi .25 caliber automatic pistol it was rusty, there was dirt adhering to the outer surfaces and could not be operated because the frame was bent and the clip was missing. The gun was bent back into place so a duplicate clip in the laboratory could be inserted into the weapon. The slide of the weapon was inoperable due to portions of the area that covers the barrel was bent. The gun was cleaned and a solution was used to remove rust. The slide and firing pin were removed from the weapon and matched up with a gun in the laboratory which was test fired. The result was test bullets which bore markings produced from the barrel, cartridge cases and firing pin of the weapon found in Chadwell Pond. When compared to the bullets found in the body of Betty Necessary and bullets taken from the trash pile it was confirmed they came from the same weapon.

The court called Ruby Cole as witness for the State. Ms. Cole is a sixth grade teacher at Kingsley Elementary School and was Betty Necessary's teacher. Mrs. Cole confirmed class was dismissed on the 26th at approximately 3:15 pm and Betty left at that time.

A side story to Ms. Cole not brought up in court and was mentioned several years later in the local newspaper Kingsport Times News showed how much she cared about her students. After the body of Betty Necessary was discovered on Saturday, Ms. Cole went back to the school and packed up Betty's personal items and returned them to Betty's parents. She knew the children would be shocked and scared so Ms. Cole positioned her desk with all the students' desks in a semi-circle around the teacher's desk and that way no student had to sit around the empty desk earlier occupied by Betty.

Walter Necessary, Betty's father, was called as witness for the State and testified the last time he saw his daughter was on February the 26th, 1970. He saw her when she left for school that day in the morning close to 7:45 am or maybe 8:00 am. Mr. Necessary identified in court clothing discovered from the crime scene and confirmed the clothing was what she had been wearing the day she disappeared. He testified that the entire family had the flu and Betty was doing the cooking and cleaning since everybody was sick. The last time he saw Betty alive was that morning before school and knew she didn't return from school that day. The next time, which was the last time he seen her was at the funeral home in her coffin.

Richard W. Flack was called as witness for the State and testified he has been a Special Agent for the FBI since 1942. He is assigned to examining soils, minerals, botanical materials and anything of a mineral nature. Mr. Flack examined the slippers and two specimens of soil from the pair of boots. The soil samples he examined were known soil samples from the cave. The soil in the cave was a yellowish-red clay type of soil. The slippers were different because they had two soils present. There was a brownish silt layer next to the sole and over this was a layer of yellowish-clay soil, which was similar to the soil identified coming from the cave. The boots also disclosed two soils which were scattered in different places on the boots. The deposits were not present in a large amount, but scattered in various places as smears and smudges and one of the soils present was a yellowish-red clay type soil which was similar to the soil identified coming from the cave. The other soil on the boots was different and could not have come from the area of the cave. Asked if the soil on the boots could positively be identified as coming from the soil from the cave, he said that based on what he seen it could have originated there but only where rare minerals could be identified could yield positive analysis be determined. He indicated there was nothing in the soil that would indicate otherwise it coming from another area, but it was possible that the soil samples at the bottom of the boots come from a different source. It would be highly unusual for soils taken from widely separated sources to be the same. The soil from the bottom of the boots was common to the area.

Special Agent Allison Simms works for the FBI, he also testified for the State he works with identification of body fluid stains, and blood stains. After examining Bowens' sweater where stains on the left sleeve and on the left front portion of the sweater were found he identified the stains as human blood stains. He also tested for semen stains on the sweater, but found nothing.

Myron T. Schoenberg, who also works for the FBI was called as witness for the State. His specialty is the hair and fiber unit doing microscopic and micro chemical examination of hairs, fibers, fabrics and related materials. Part of the evidence he was presented with was pubic hairs belonging to the victim and also the defendant, Fred Bowen. By using a comparison microscope with a magnifying possibility of 1,190 times compared the unknown hairs found on the victim with the hairs of the defendant and they were identical. He explained that a hair can have up to approximately 16 identifiable characteristics. All hairs may not have these characteristics and lack these characteristics. Hair has 3 main parts, the outside part called the cuticle, the middle part is the cortex and middle part is called the medulla. The outside is covered with scales that can either lay flat or protrude and can also have different lengths and depths, can be thick or thin. The cuticle also determines the color which can vary shades. The cortex contains the pigment; this gives hair its color. The pigment exists in granules- granular shapes which can be round, rectangular, big or small. In the cortex you can also find little air spaces called cortical fusi, which can either be or not be present. The medulla can be thick or thin, interrupted or un-interrupted. According to the witness, the hairs were identical and could have come from the defendant; however, hairs do not contain enough identifying characteristics to be positively identified as coming from one certain individual. Since the hairs could not be positively identified as belonging to Fred Bowen- the hairs examined were determined to be microscopically identical. Mr. Scholberg also testified that the hairs found inside of the victim's vagina did not originate from the victim- they were not microscopically identical.

Another item examined which was taken from Fred Bowen was a brown sweater and the garment was hung upside down on a scrapping table by hooking and allowed to hang freely while a piece of brown wrapping paper was placed below the sweater and using a plain kitchen spatula the sweater was scraped down lightly. Any debris on the sweater may fall on the paper and each piece of debris is collected with a brief description of the debris and labeled for any future identification. He was asked to examine items to see if there was an interchange of fibers and hairs between the clothing of the suspect and the victim. Several items of clothing were scraped using the same technique as the sweater. He could identify fibers that matched the brown wool sweater that the defendant owned on the victim's belongings. Fibers from the sweater were also found on the gag and material that appeared to be a shirt used both as a gag and to tie the victims' hands. When asked about the number of fibers found his answer ranged from "many" to "several" on the materials used as bindings. The T-shirt material used as a gag listed "many" for the material used as a gag which was a piece of T-shirt material. The final gag, which was inside the victim's mouth only had a "few" matching fibers from the sweater on it. When asked about the number of fibers on the victim's clothing some of the victim's clothing was listed as "several" however the slacks had "many" fibers on them. When asked about positive identification he testified that, much like hair a positive identification cannot be made of wool therefore he definitely cannot say that the fibers came from the garment.

When Mr. McInturff interviewed Mr. Scholberg regarding the positive analysis of a hair, he testified that a hair could not be positively identified as coming from an individual however you can rule out a certain individual. He can say that with the aid of a comparison microscope you can compare fibers and either match them or eliminate them. He has made ten thousand examinations since he came to the lab and maybe four or five times he could not differentiate between the hair of a suspect and a victim. Mr. Scholberg was asked about identifying hair on the body, he explained he could primarily divide the hair into three areas for identification: the pubic area; the head area and the limb area. The debris collected from the items made of material was placed in a pillbox and after he removed the hairs and fibers he put the pill boxes in a plastic envelope and returned them with the other evidence to the Sullivan County Sheriff.

Richard W. Flack was called as witness for the State since he handled the examination of fingernail scrapings for the victim. There were two particles found in the nail scrapings of yellowish red clay, which compared to the clay at the cave and a little tiny plant particle which appeared to be a very, small fragment of a stem; however nothing else under the nails was found. The nail scrapings were also checked for blood, tissue or flesh but nothing else could be found.

One of the witnesses for the State was Paul N. Fox who works for the Kingsport National Bank on New Beason Well Road not far from the Bloomingdale Grill. Mr. Fox testified that he saw Freddie on the 26th of February but was not sure of the exact time and couldn't say for sure if it was during lunch because he lived not far from the bank and sometimes he would go home for lunch. He went down to the grill later on in the day around 5:10 pm when he and his wife ate at there for supper. When they went into the grill they seen Freddie Bowen and he was parked outside the grill in his car by himself sitting upright but partially slumped over the steering wheel. Mr. Fox spoke with Freddie, but Freddie did not speak back at him.

Both Mr. Fox and his wife had ordered their food and about 5 minutes has passed when he noticed the car that Fred was in had left, but he did not see him leave.

David Conner was the next to be called as witness on behalf of the Defendant and he was examined by Mr. McInturff. Mr. Conner testified that he lives in Bloomingdale, and works at Kingsport Press. Mr. Conner testified that he knew Freddie Bowen and was not related to him. He was asked if he remembered the day the little Necessary girl went missing and he indicated that he did, he recalled that he was in the Bloomingdale Grill and he saw Freddis Bowen that day around 4:20 to 4:25. David was there shooting pool with Donnie Bowen, who is a friend to him.

After his brief encounter with Fred he did not see him again that day; Fred left the grlll about 5 or 10 minutes before he did. David Conner was cross examined by General Kirkpatrick, who asked about how often he frequented the grill and he said he was there at the grill a lot. He told the court he was friends with Donnie and Marvin both, but considered Donnie to be his best friend. He knew that Donnie and Marvin were brothers. He knew Andrew Bowen, who was both Donnie and Marvin's father and considered him to be a good friend. On the evening of February 26, 1970 he and Donnie got there about the same time, possibly he got there before Donnie. He shot pool with Donnie for about 15 minutes and also got something to eat, then he left shortly after because Donnie and his father had to Johnson City to pick up a car.

Mr. Conner stated that when he left the grill that day Marvin and his wife were operating the business. General Kirkpatrick questioned Mr. Conner to whether Andrew, Marvin and Donnie were in the pool table area of the restaurant and if they could they have seen Fred if he was there and he confirmed they would have. General Kirkpatrick questioned Mr. Conner when Andrew Bowen first approached him about remembering what happened while they're at the grill on Thursday and he said that he was not for sure, but to the best of his recollection it was on Friday sometime, which would have been February 27th, 1970. Mr. Conner said that he had stopped in the grill on Friday and he was questioned about whether that he had seen Donnie or Freddie while he was in the grill and he confirmed that he had seen both of them. Final comment from Mr. Conner was that it was Friday or Saturday that the Bowen's were asking him about seeing Freddie in the grill, but it was before the discovery of Betty Jean's body.

General Kirkpatrick asked him if the Bowen's normally questioned him like that and he told the court they normally didn't. General Kirkpatrick asked Mr. Conner if he was at the grill on both Friday and Saturday and he confirmed he was. He was asked if he

remembered if Fred was there at the grill on Friday or Saturday

and he said not as far as he knew. He was asked about Wednesday,

February 25th, whether or not he had seen Fred that day and Mr.

Conner responded that he remembered Fred being there about the

same time he was there. He was asked about other days that Fred

was present and some he wasn't sure about because he either

couldn't' remember or wasn't there at the café

Marvin Bowen was called on behalf of the defendant by Mr.

McInturff. He confirmed that he knew Freddie Bowen and that he

remembered the day the Necessary girl disappeared. He saw

Freddie that day at the Bloomingdale Grill between 5:00 pm and

5:15 pm- he guessed. When he saw him, he was sitting in his car

alone in front of the grill and again about 6:30 that same day. Mr.

Bowen told the court that Paul Fox, who worked for the bank was

there at the grill with his wife and kids about 5:00-5:15. Mr.

Bowen had no conversations with Freddie when he was in his car.

Fred stayed in his car for about 10 minutes. That was the only time

he remembered Fred being at the grill that day. The attorney asked if his father, Andrew Bowen was there at the grill and he said that he was not. He had to go pick up some papers for an automobile and also to Tom Dossett's office. He said that Donnie was with his father. Andrew and Donnie left about 4:00-4:30 pm and they had been at the grill until then. He said there are so many customers coming in and out during the dinner hour and he didn't know exact times for either Fred or Andrew. He was asked when he worked at the grill and he said that it varied, sometimes at 11:00 and work until 2:00 and come back maybe around 3:00. He said that it was probably around 3:30 when he came back to work for his dad. After Marvin Bowen testified Dr. Shelton Gelburd was sworn in. Dr. Gelburd is a Psychologist. The jury was asked to leave while the Court and attorneys determined whether that his testimony should be used because Fred Bowen the defendant had entered a plea of not guilty; however to use the testimony it would bring up the issue of sanity. The question of sanity or insanity can't be shown under the general plea of not guilty. It was determined that the questions to Dr. Gelburd would be limited to, the condition during the alleged offense. It was not a question of sanity or insanity since it was not raised in the manner required.

Shelton Gelburd was called as witness on behalf of the Defendant; he is a Clinical Psychologist working one day in Kingsport and the remainder of the week in Knoxville, Tennessee at Psychiatric Services. He worked at the Eastern State Mental Hospital in Knoxville from 1962 to 1965. In the last 5 years has examined 3,000 people and saw Freddie Bowen as a patient. He saw Fred three (3) times at 132 West Sevier Avenue in Kingsport, TN. This was with the cooperation of the Sheriff's Department- they brought him down there. Dr. Gelburd's profession was specifically concerned with human maladjustment, human thinking, disturbances, human emotional disturbances and disturbances in behavior. He administered four (4) different tests: The Rorschach (ink blot- widely used personality test); Wechsler Adult Intelligence Scale (IQ Test); The Benton Visual Retention test (tests of organic brain damage); Draw a Person test (test of personality). Two major subheadings for the IQ test is verbal which deals mainly with thinking, talking, conceptualizing and a performance section deals mainly with skills and manipulating things like fixing a car or tying a shoelace. His verbal score was 73 and 100 is normal. His performance IQ is 84 and again normal is 100. The score of 73 is borderline, which is dull normal- below normal and mentally defective. The performance score of 84 is also considered dull normal. Dr. Gelburd spent approximately 3.5 hours with Freddie- he talked to him mainly to get an impression of what kind of person he was. He also spoke with Andrew Bowen which is Freddie's half-brother. The results of the test strongly give evidence of organic brain damage. Dr. Gelburd had a very extensive part of training in the brain and with brain damage. Since intelligence is affected by brain damage the test is designed to weed out what functions might be affected by brain damage. The test revealed a strong evidence of brain damage. After reviewing a history it was determined that Fred had suffered traumatic injury to his head on at least three (3) occasions. He was in two (2) car wrecks in which he was hit in the head and hospitalized and he was in a bicycle accident in which he was thrown 20 to 25 feet and fell on his head on the asphalt. The dates that Dr. Gelburd met with

Fred were on June 19, 1970, June 27, 1970 and July 3, 1970. Dr. Gelburd was asked by Mr. McInturff if he knew what psychomotor epilepsy, schizophrenia and hallucination means and he explained each one. "Psychomotor epilepsy is an alteration in one's state of consciousness due to brain dysfunction, which clouds his awareness of the world, produces a warped view of the world, produces imaginary objects in the world and as a result the individual might perceive tremendous danger to himself when it does not exist and actually lose control of himself, not know what he was doing and might hurt someone". Dr. Gelburd explained that brain damage handles psychomotor epilepsy and brain damage can lead to an uncovering of schizophrenia. Dr. Gelburd also testified there is strong evidence that Freddie is suffering from schizophrenia. During the questioning, Dr. Gelburd was asked by Mr. MacIntuff what effect that alcohol has on the brain of an individual with brain damage and he responded it could release an underlying psychosis. The question of a raised body temperature of an individual with brain damage and Dr. Gelburd responded that a raised body temperature could release a behavioral problem. On a

125

normal brain it would take a higher temperature to release a

behavioral problem. This applied to general situations, but not

every specific case. Fred had incurred injuries to his head, which

easily could have produced brain damage. He had been drinking

liquor the day of Betty's abduction and he had an elevated body

temperature since he was suffering from the flu. Dr. Gelburd was

asked by Mr. MacIntuff if while he examined Freddie Bowen; in

his opinion are there periods he might know the difference between

right and wrong and the doctor answered "yes". He also asked if it

could also be true for February 26th and he answered "yes". Dr.

Gelburd answered the question when asked by General

Kirkpatrick if he knew whether Fred Bowen knew right from

wrong on Feb. 26, 1970- "I think only God could".

Burt Anderson was called as Witness for the Defendant and she is

employed by the Sullivan County Board of Education Office. Miss

Anderson was asked if the records she had in court with her part of

the official records kept in the Superintendent's office under the

Department of Education for Sullivan County at which she

responded that it was. She confirmed that the school system gave

IQ tests as a matter of standard procedure. Ms. Anderson brought with her the record for the last year that Freddie Bowen attended school. During questioning, she answered that she did not have with her the Achievement Test only the IQ test for Freddie Bowen administered in 1956 and 1957 school year. The results of his IQ test was 66. He was chronological age 12 years and 7 months; however the mental age was 7 years and 11 months. This is a difference of 5 years in mental age. When this test was given Freddie was in the fifth grade and in the first month of school, he made an "F" in each subject. The second month, six "F's", one "C" and one "D". The next month, six "F's", two "C's". He dropped out of school in March- the month beginning March 25th after three (3) days and did not re-enter. She had in her possession the "Lorge-Thorndike Intelligence Test" which was commonly given. The student is asked questions and you would give a mark for your answer. If your reading was not very good, then somebody couldn't take the test if Freddie could not read and write, then the results would reflect a lower score.

REBUTTAL- Roger K. White was called as a witness on behalf of the State- Direct Examination by General Kirkpatrick. Stated that he is a Medical Doctor and a Psychiatrist. Dr. White examined Freddie Bowen when he was received at the Maximum Security Division of Central State Psychiatric Hospital. He examined him at the request of the Department of Mental Health by staff members on July 6, 1970, and July 13, 1970. He was examined by a staff physician and given a physical. A psychiatric history was obtained by one of the staff physicians. Psychiatric history and examination was conducted by Dr. White personally. Psychological testing was carried out by a member of the staff Psychologist. An electroencephalogram was done; x-rays of the chest and skull were performed. A routine blood count with urinalysis which is part of the admission procedure was also done. Various routine tests were performed and a history was obtained from the Eastern State Psychiatric Hospital they did from October 5, 1962 to January 28, 1963. The request was done at the request of a court in another county for pre-trial evaluation. Other staff examined Fred and Dr. Roger White testified that he found nothing that would consider indicative of brain damage. He is illiterate and cannot read but he could find no usual impairment seen with brain damage. He also found no other abnormalities with Mr. Bowen. He was asked if Fred was mentally ill and Dr. White answered "No". He was asked if in his opinion Fred knew the difference between right and wrong and he answered "Yes". There is nothing in the tests or examination, he performed to indicate that he did not know right from wrong on Feb. 26, 1970.

Dr. White was cross examined by Mr. McInturff who asked when a man develops a knowledge of right and wrong and Dr. White testified that it was somewhere around the age of 1. According to Roger White it is possible for a man to have brain damage and it doesn't show up on the electrical encephalogram (EEG). The explanation for this is the man may have a tumor or brain cancer and it not show up on the EEG. Psychological tests are very poor for brain damage; the best indexes of brain damage come in psychiatric examination. A person's memory is a clear index of brain damage- to be exact, recent memory. While being examined by the doctor, he gave the usual responses to the ink blot test and was cooperative, but gave the usual popular responses or a fair number of "I don't know the answers".

Robert Small was called as witness for the State, he is the owner of Small Jewelers on 109 West Market Street in Kingsport, TN. Todd and Dossett Law Office is located upstairs from Small Jewelers. Before he moved his jewelry shop he was located upstairs across the hall from Todd and Dossett. Mr. Small was asked if he knew Fred Bowen and he answered that Fred had been in his shop before and would come in regularly until either December or January for Mr. Small to do odds and ends on jewelry he owned. He told the court that when he seen Fred in court it was the first time he had seen him in a long while. He said that Fred tried to trade jewelry with him often, but most of the time he would have Mr. Small clean jewelry or repair work on jewelry he owned. Mr. Small was nervous while being questioned on the stand. When he was asked Mr. Small did not recollect Fred coming into his shop in February. He insisted that he saw him somewhere around Christmas and forgot seeing him in February, still his response sounded unsure of the possibility. He was asked about whether that he traded with

Fred and he said that Fred normally brought in jewelry to be repaired or cleaned and could find no record of him being in and trading with him and he clarified that trading was not just when Fred would buy from him but also referred to Fred bringing in jewels for Mr. Small to purchase. Mr. MacIntuff asked Mr. Small, who he referred to as "Robert" whether or not that he purchased any diamonds worth $5,000 from him and Mr. Small advised the court he had not. The interesting point of this testimony is that Mr. Small had already testified that he had not seen Fred in his shop since either December or January; however, when he was asked again about him seeing any diamonds that Fred might have brought in his shop February 1970, he said that he did not recall seeing any diamonds- he didn't remember seeing them so who was "them". He was questioned by Mr. MacIntuff if any, other places downtown was about the same size as his shop and he answered "yes" and when asked about if he knew of any other jewelry shops next to Tom Dossett, upstairs (as his shop was) he answered "no". Bob Moore was called as witness for the State and he is with the Kingsport Police Department. Mr. Moore testified that he was with

Freddie Bowen for about 30 minutes, taking pictures, fingerprints, and history. He observed no scratches, etc. on his forehead which would indicate that his wife had hit him as she claimed. Since Freddie was booked on Saturday and the altercation took place on Thursday any scratches or bruises may not have been visible.

Dr. William A. Wiley is the Associate Medical Examiner in the Kingsport area and pointed out when he testified that he did not perform the actual autopsy; however, he was present and witnessed as Dr. Harrison performed the procedure. Dr. Wiley was called on February 28th to the morgue at the Holston Valley Community Hospital to examine the body of Betty Jean Necessary.

Dr. Wiley described the body as a 12 year old girl, weighing approximately 105 pounds and was about five feet tall. There was a bluish discoloration over the entire surface of the body on the front and back. Examination of the body revealed four gunshot wounds of the upper back and evidence of trauma to the left nipple. Closer examination of the trauma to the nipple was determined to be the exit wound of one of the bullets. A fifth bullet wound was in the right lower abdomen, landing in the buttocks on the left side.

The victim had been gagged thoroughly and arms tied behind her back. Examination of the opening of the vagina revealed definite evidence of extensive lacerations of the vagina with the old blood present. The hymeneal ring had been torn and extended into the posterior vaginal mucosa, meaning a tear in the back where the vaginal membrane is located. There were multiple tears to the hymeneal ring, and it was noted the vaginal lacerations were extensive. The doctor was asked about the injuries to this area of the body and he testified the injuries would be painful. There was also a laceration to the skull, which at first was thought to be superficial, but upon closer inspection revealed the wound penetrated all the way to the bone although it did not penetrate into the brain.

Tests on vaginal secretions indicated strong positive for acid phosphates one of the constituents found in semen.

Dr. William Harrison was called as a witness for the State and he was identified as a pathologist for the Holston Valley Community

Hospital. Dr. Harrison has been with the hospital and practicing

Pathology for 18 years. He explained to the court that pathology is

the study of cause and effects of diseases of the human body. Dr.

Harrison was educated at Yale University Medical School, was in

the residence program at Yale University at the University of

Pennsylvania and Board certified in Pathology. He examined the

body of Betty Jean Necessary in the autopsy room at the Holston

Valley Community Hospital to determine the extent of injuries and

cause of death. Dr. Harrison was asked to describe the condition of

the body and to describe the wound to the victim's head. Dr.

Harrison testified that he saw the child before the gag was taken

out of her mouth and he was shown pictures of the victim and

asked if that accurately depicted the condition of the body which

he confirmed. Dr. Harrison was asked to describe the head wound

and he told the court; it was a clean cut all the way through the

scalp about a half an inch in length and it went down to the bone

but caused no fracture to the skull. The wound to the head would

have been a painful injury.

Dr. Harrison was asked if he examined the private parts of the child, which he confirmed and explained that she had a tear in the lower part of the entrance to her vagina and there was blood around this area. There were bruises over the upper part of the entrance, over the pelvic bone and bruises of the soft tissues. The bruises were in the area called a pubis consistent with forcible body contacts in particular forcible sexual intercourse. When asked if any scars was inside her body that would indicate that she had ever had prior sexual experience he said there was no evidence. Dr. Harrison performed a test to determine whether acid phosphatase was present in her body which is a chemical test for an enzyme found in the male sexual secretion in the prostate. The result was a strong positive. Although acid phosphatase was found sperm was not found; however sperm only exists inside the body for a short period before it deteriorates. The normal time frame for this to begin is after a few hours and usually not over 24 hours. Dr. Harrison explained that he is not aware of a way to test and determine whether sperm was present before they break down. To his knowledge, there is no other way for acid phosphatase to be present in a woman's body other than the exposure of sperm.

Dr. Harrison described the bullet wounds in the victim's body-there were two bullet wounds in the front part of the body. One was an exit wound and the other was an entrance wound. The entrance wound was on the lower abdomen to the right of the belly button. This bullet went down thru the abdominal cavity rearward and downwards and ended in the left buttock. The wound would not have been fatal, but it would have been very painful because it shattered bone in the pelvis extensively on the left side and any breaking of the bone is very painful. The bleeding of this wound wouldn't have been excessive, but it bled both internally and externally. There were four bullet wounds in the victim's back. The bullet in the buttock was recovered and given to Johnny Robertson by the Sheriff's Department. The other bullets were identified on a chart as numbers 1-4. Bullet number 1 was the highest one on the right and it entered just thru the shoulder blade bone and went upward more or less to the head and forward lodging in the front part of the body near the shoulder bone on the right in the shoulder tissues in front. Bullet number 2 was lower down and the second one down near the midline, crossed the midline, went thru the lung and lodged in the upper part of the neck tissues on the left crossing the midline. Bullet number 3 followed a similar course was slightly below the second bullet and followed a parallel course, went thru the lung and entered the lower part of the neck. This bullet lodged up a little farther out again in front of the shoulder bone. Bullet number 4 was the lowest and last bullet went thru the lung on the left side and is the bullet that exited through the nipple of the left breast and this bullet was not located. The other three bullets were found and these were also given to Johnny Robertson by the Sheriff's Department. Dr. Harrison also conducted an internal examination of the body and during this examination, he found 3 hairs deep inside her body. The hairs were located high inside of the vagina and they were found from the inside, not from the outside. Hair does not grow in that area of the human body, therefore the hair had to come from outside of the body. When asked how long the victim could have lived after being shot 5 times as indicated and also taking in consideration of the other wounds on the body, he explained that he could not be for certain but felt it would be a relatively short while, probably minutes. It is hard to estimate how long even in minutes because different factors, but it could vary from less than a minute to few or several minutes. When asked about what pain that the victim would have been in Dr. Harrison explained that, assuming the victim was conscious the wounds would be very painful wounds because of the extent of the directions of them and they penetrated so deeply in the body. The most painful injury probably was the one in the pelvis. The effect of the gag on the victim's body would have prevented the victim from expelling the blood which would have been coming up through the throat and be present in the mouth. Since the bullet wounds went through the lung tissues, there would be bleeding within the lung. According to Dr. Harrison the cause of the victim's death was bullet wounds through the lungs which penetrated many blood vessels in the lung and the victim bled. Due to the bleeding into her chest internally caused her to drown in her own blood. When Mr. McInturff interviewed Dr. Harrison he asked about her time of death. Dr.

Harrison explained that he could estimate her death within certain limits. After the victim has been dead for over 24 hours it makes it more difficult to determine the time of death. The victim was examined by Dr. Harrison on February 28, 1970 at approximately 4-4:30 pm which was shortly after she was found. In Dr. Harrison's opinion the victim most likely had been dead over 24 hours. The most reliable method of determining death is body temperature. After a victim has been dead for over 24 hours it is speculation to a certain degree on the time of death. Rigor mortis will commence about 4 hours after death, depending on external factors, condition of the body, whether or not the body is under stress, if the victim was a muscular person, and age. The stress that Dr. Harrison is referring to is mental stress, such as a sudden emergency and physical stress. The physical stress would affect the metabolism and muscles and developing rigor. After 24 hours, rigor is of no help in determining the time of death because the body would have no reflex rigor. Stress or shock will impair and sometimes causes digestion to stop. Narrowing down a time of death, sometimes can also be made difficult because of other

139

factors involved, such as environmental, temperature and so forth. Dr. Harrison was questioned about whether the victim could have died on Friday the 27th to which he responded that he couldn't say categorically that she could not have but he didn't think so. Asked about if she could have died up to 8:00 pm on Thursday February 26th and he said that it was possible, but that the questioning was in a range of where he couldn't make an hourly differentiation. Dr. Harrison testified that he could not make a determination if the victim died at 3 o'clock or 8 o'clock on the 26th since the meal in her system was not digested and could have been delayed by stress. General Kirkpatrick questioned Dr. Harrison again about the head wound he testified the injury was caused not by a blunt object but by a sharp object. The gun that caused the bullet wounds could also have caused the head wound. The time of death was discussed again and Dr. Harrison said nothing indicated that the victim died on any other date than February 26, 1970, however he could not say for sure the exact time.

Arguments- General Calhoun- Pointed out that it was a typical February afternoon, not rainy and was not especially bad weather.

Fred Bowen and his brother in law had been to Virginia earlier that day to purchase cigarettes and they came back to Bloomingdale Grill which seemed to be a point they always returned. Phillip Laforce got out of the vehicle and left with a boy named Johnny Riley, who is a friend of Phillip's. It was approximately 2 miles from Andrew's restaurant to the Laforce home. While Mrs. Laforce was watching her afternoon soap operas, Sandra was there and a child- which was Sandra's brother Tim was also present. They said that Fred grabbed off a roll or part of a roll of pink paper towels and left the house to go up on the hill to the bathroom and then to do some shooting. This was about 2:00 in the afternoon and he was not seen again until about 4:30. The hill up from the Laforce house goes into the woods that adjoined the home of Betty Necessary. There was evidence that Fred used the bathroom in the area above the cave where Officer J.C. Fletcher found the stained brown, pink paper towels.

The teacher, Ruby Cole told the court that Betty Jean got out of school at 3:15 that day. Betty stayed at Wanda Hickman's house for a few minutes witnessed by Mrs. Begley, who saw her go in the house and said that Betty stayed for only a few minutes, she couldn't have been inside the Begley home over 2 minutes. She went thru the residential lots and then walked up the road about 3:42pm. This area is only about a two minute walk to the wooded area in the road. From that time she saw nobody else except for her killer(s). From the thickly wooded section where the road turns, her books were found just a short distance in the thickest part of the woods. No articles of clothing or anything else was found there- just her books. An old road bed goes up, but it doesn't go in a straight line it comes around and passes, goes over to the cave, to the area also where the clothes were found, which is between the place where the books were found, and the cave. The evidence develops to where you can find that was the place where Betty Jean Necessary was assaulted and raped. Her undergarments, pantyhose, pants, remaining portion of her bell bottom slacks, parts of her blouse, and the remaining section of a piece of what appeared to be a man's T-shirt material were found. The piece of T-shirt material had brown stains or brown looking spots on it.

Two to three hundred yards away is the cave and a natural depression. The body of Betty Necessary was covered with leaves and dirt and some brush pushed over her. Only a small part of her hands and a small part of the back of her body was visible. Her condition as far as we can determine was that she had her bra pulled down, one strap broken, and was hanging around her waist. Part of her blouse was hanging around her waist, her hands tied behind her, an inner gag made of T-shirt material in her mouth, two (2) other gags of T-shirt material and then finally a strip of her bell bottom trousers on the outer part of that. Her bell bottom trousers were at the scene where her other clothing was that is, where her underclothes were found. Her clothes were not removed as normally you would remove clothes because there was no reason- her clothes were ripped from her body, then she was assaulted near what was to be her grave at the entrance to a cave. It is unknown whether she was partially gagged or partially bound, but the last gag went on her where she was raped- the last gag. The last gag was the part of her bell bottom trousers, where the remaining pieces of the pants were found. The last piece of T-shirt material was used perhaps by the killer to clean himself off after he raped her. It didn't take long, to get from the road where she was abducted on Kingsley Avenue to where the clothes were found. He rushed her to the point of the assault and then he rushed her from the point of the assault to the cave after he had placed the coat over Betty and buttoned one button.

It can only be estimated that she walked that distance with her hands tied behind her after she had been assaulted, terror stricken, and no doubt in great pain. She was in great pain because of the extent of her injuries found on her female organs. At some point Betty was shot in the front and it was a very painful gunshot wound, excruciating pain, because part of her pelvis was fractured by that gunshot wound. Perhaps she was hit over the head, but again why would she have been hit over the head at this point? It would have been pointless since the killer had already shot her once, why not just finish her off then? It is not known where she received the blow to her head, only that she received a blow to her head, which went all the way through to the skull. The body was found down on her knees slumped over and four (4) bullet wounds in the back. It is probably reasonable to assume that she was finished off there. It is unknown if she died immediately or how long that she lived, was she alive when the killer(s) raked the dirt and leaves over her body- probably. The next people to see Fred was Mrs. Laforce and his wife, Sandra Laforce who said that the defendant came out of the woods about 4:30 pm approximately. He walked out of the woods into the yard and just stared at the ground. Later on Mrs. Laforce heard a pecking sound, and that is when she found Fred at the cinder block pile beating something on the cinder block white in color; he got in his car and left.

The newspaper lady who was there that day collecting money for the paper said that she got there about 5:00 or maybe a little after 5:00. She also saw him jump into his car and leave, he goes to Bloomingdale Grill, which was about two miles- about three minutes from where he was at. He was seen by another witness who fixes his time at 5:05 to 5:15- the witness was the banker Paul Fox. Marvin Bowen, his nephew said he also saw him and he was in his car and appeared to be sick, slumped over his steering wheel just a little. The banker spoke with Fred; however Fred does not speak back to him. After a short time, then Mr. Fox recalled it was not over 5 minutes that Fred left the grill. Not long after he leaves the grill he goes to the home of Rose Dunn and he blows the horn-this is right down from the Laforce home and both Sandra and her mother heard the horn blowing. Phillip was at the Dunn house when he heard a horn blowing so he goes outside to see what it wrong and it is Freddie. There is something definitely wrong with Freddie Bowen; he wants to tell somebody something. Phillip gets in the car, Freddie is a little bit sick and he tells Phillip he killed somebody. He tells Phillip he was out target practicing up on the hill he shot into a bush, the person fell and they died and they were dead when he got there and it was accidental. When Phillip's eyes got big then he told them he was just kidding, "you take everything seriously". He then tells Phillip they need to get some whiskey and they head for the liquor store located on the Super Highway. Phillip goes into the liquor store and gets two (2) fifths of whiskey with money given to him by Fred. While Phillip was in the liquor store, Fred was trying to help a man start his car; then after Phillip got back outside they go back to Andrew Bowen's grill.

Fred and Phillip got back to the grill about 6:30 pm per Marvin and Fred had been drinking and was so drunk that his half-brother Andrew took the keys away from him. Andrew wasn't that opposed to drinking because he went out to Fred's car and poured some of the liquor in glasses. Andrew was responsible enough to know that Freddie didn't need to be driving so he took the keys away from him and the car sat there at his grill until the next day. The defendant and his brother in law walked home when his wife saw him with Phillip when she was on her way to wash clothes at the Laundry Mat. She had her friend drive her to where Fred was and there was a fuss between Sandra and Fred in the middle of the road. The fuss was so bad that one of the neighbors turned the porch light on and words exchanged between Fred and the neighbor that continued until Fred threatened to shoot the light out at the neighbor's house. He told Sandra they could not live together any longer and they had to break up. When she asked why they had to break up, he told Sandra he had killed somebody. Sandra is not exactly sure of what he was talking about or why he was saying what he did and it is also possible that she does not

147

want to remember it the way she does. Sandra recalled they had a disagreement earlier that morning about a red headed girl that had caused conflict between them.

The next day Fred goes to pick up his car at the grill and it was 11:00 am- or closer to noon. Fred's wife does not want to remember what happened so her testimony cannot be taken seriously, but you can tell by Sandra's testimony she has no doubt about what occurred.

Mr. McInturff pointed out that one man couldn't have been the only one that abducted, raped and killed Betty Necessary because if Fred had a gun then how did he tie the knots? Whoever tied the knots had to have used both hands and couldn't have done the things without using both hands. He also pointed out that he didn't know who all was involved in the crime, but knew that it would take a lot longer while than the proof shows in the record and he was confident of that. The Laforces had a reason to lie if necessary because their son, Phillip Laforce was first accused of the crime and was taken downtown and questioned. It was not denied that the sweater belonged to Phillip, although the boots were denied as belonging to him. Why did it take so long to locate the boots right on top of the road? There were police out there in numbers looking at the house and they were looking for the gun. What officer could have failed to look in the ditch line and miss the boots, especially considering that the tile was not hidden, it only had a little grass over it so nothing could have prevented them from discovering the boots during the 5 day period where the boots remained in the tile. Fred Bowen was in jail by the time the boots were discovered. How did they get in there and how were they failed to be found? Who could have been in the vicinity that would have an interest in the boots being found? The vehicle that belonged to Fred Bowen was there and could have been searched so why wasn't it? According to Mr. McInturff, there is an alternative to capital punishment which would be life in prison. We can correct a prison sentence, but we cannot correct taking a man's life. He mentioned that the "good book" tells us not to take a human life. By condemning Fred to die he tried to imply that Fred would meet the jurors "on the other side". He asked the jurors not to let District

Attorney Carl Kirkpatrick's opinion and what he had on Fred

Bowen influence them into executing Fred Bowen.

General Kirkpatrick's closing argument: He wanted to point out

and discuss things that were important to their family, children and

people of the County and State. Nobody is asking the jury to go out

there and erect a scaffold and hang the man or to set up an electric

chair and pull the switch. They are asking them to perform a

function of the system. The death penalty is in place to protect

society and has been around since the beginning of time. The jury

is not there to seek vengeance, but to see that justice is served. The

defendant denied 4 times he owned a .25 caliber pistol. This gun is

the same gun he attempted to trade to Bud Adams. The boots

found were a size 9 1/2 D which is the same size that Fred wears.

The trousers he wore that day, which should have been blood

soaked are missing. The shoe size that Phillip Laforce wears is a

size 7 which his mother testified that he wore. Fred more than

likely had no reason to cover up for Phillip Laforce.

General Kirkpatrick mentioned that no blood or skin was found

under the nails of Betty Jean and he also indicated there was no other scratches, cuts, etc. to her body other than her private parts. Fred already had the gags ready and was waiting for Betty- he left the Laforce house at 2:00 pm and went into the woods. Sandra established that Fred got home around 4:30 pm- which could be off a little on the time. He left immediately after getting home and went to the Bloomingdale Grill where Mr. Fox the banker saw him over there between 5:10 and 5:15 pm. The strongest evidence suggests that Fred got to the Laforce home around 5:00 pm and that he left the gun there at the house, stood outside for a while and then drove over to the grill and arrived about 5:10 pm. Mr. Fox said that he left no longer than 5 minutes later when he saw Fred and he was slumped over in his car. By slumping over in the car seat this indicated he was sick about what he had done. He went back and got Phillip then went to the liquor store. The Conner man said that he was right there at the grill while Andrew, Donnie, Mrs. Bowen and Marvin was there. Mrs. Bowen may have seen him. But Andrew was there talking to him with Donnie and Marvin. Mr. Conner's is mistaken about his time because he didn't know what time and day he was there at the Bloomingdale Grill. He was not

151

sure when Marvin started first asking him about seeing Fred there
if it was Friday or Saturday and this was before the child's body
was discovered, nobody had even pointed a finger at Fred yet.
Betty's body was discovered about 11:00 pm on Saturday which
they all testified to so why was the Bowen's questioning Mr.
Conner about seeing Freddie?

Fred testified that he had been downtown to see Robert Small and
Mr. Small testified that Fred had been in the shop before and had
shown him the diamonds. Fred owns and operates a late model
Pontiac Bonneville, which is a much better vehicle than many
people owned. Fred is not brilliant but he falls in the same general
category as a quarter of the population that can maintain a normal
life without killing other people. Why did Fred hide the boots, the
trousers and why did he throw the gun in the pond if he had
nothing to hide? Does this show, you a killer or just a man trying
to cover up a crime? It shows to most people he knew what he was
doing was wrong and the only thing you have to look at is the
facts.

The jury was asked to decide based on facts and also for Betty, who did not reach her home that day. She was full of hope and full of promise was she was brutally raped and murdered. She was raped and after having to suffer the indignity of such a crime her coat was placed on her shoulders, which her arms still bound behind her and she was walking to the grave – to the hole called a cave and then she was shot in the stomach. With the excruciating pain that the wound would have caused she could not grab like you would normally do if you were hit in a place like that because her hands were bound tightly behind her back. She fell forward and then had four more bullets pumped into her body (her back) while she was bent over. This is the best theory since nobody was there that could testify what exactly happened. She did not die in dignity and she did not die instantly. She died cruelly, slowly, naked and in pain on the cold February afternoon. Naked with her hands bound behind her back with a gag in her mouth. She didn't even have the ability to clear the blood from her lungs drowning her- that is how she died. Why was she killed- it was to keep this man from having to face everybody in court on a charge of rape. Betty

153

Jean Necessary was sentenced to death by Fred Bowen to cover up his crime of rape- he wanted to save his own skin. She cannot take the witness stand and that is why she is dead. This murder is not an ordinary murder. This isn't a murder building up from a long hatred, bad blood, fights and scrapes building up over time. This was the murder of an innocent child, a sixth grade innocent child. By his own lack of remorse, Fred has affixed the proper penalty of death for himself. There would be an easy way out by giving him a life sentence, however that would not be just. The verdict must be fair to the people of the county, fair to the family of Betty Jean, to the other children and most of all to Betty Jean. Had the defendant taken the stand and had told the court he did it, was sorry or even couldn't remember doing it and shown remorse then it would be different. He has not asked for mercy? The only thing he is sorry for is that he got caught.

Charge of the Court: The jury is told that the indictment charges the defendant with the crime of murder in the 1st degree and includes murder in the second degree, voluntary manslaughter and involuntary manslaughter.

During the trial security was important and it was common for deputies to be stationed on both sides of all doors. Freddie Bowen has remained in an isolation cell at the Sullivan County Jail since his arrest on the day the body of Betty Necessary was found.

The trial was over within 6 days and the jury was out only 2 hours. That time included the jury eating lunch.

On July 25, 1970 Fred J. Bowen was convicted of 1st degree murder of abducting an elementary school age child; who he raped & tortured. Afterward, he fired bullets into her body and then buried her alive. This crime was defined by the newspaper as "the most brutal crime imaginable". Bowen, who held no emotion during this trial blinked twice, then looked down on the desktop, he returned his gaze back to the jury while the verdict was read and made no comments and showed no emotion.

Fred J. Bowen was sentenced to death by electrocution. Finally the mother of Betty Necessary that had remained so strong during the trial, even during the most brutal details of the crime could cry her composure finally giving in to thoughts of her beloved child. One important footnote is that Betty's father had clarified it during the trial, he did not want the death penalty for Fred because it was against his religion.

There were none of the expected outbursts in the courtroom only the low murmurs that radiated throughout the courtroom.

Mr. McInturff in a dramatic plea asked for the jury not to invoke the death penalty because the case was primarily based on "circumstantial evidence". According to Mr. McInturff there were no eyewitnesses to this crime, but District Attorney Carl Kirkpatrick said it best when he said later there was no eye witnesses since Fred took the only eyewitness to this crime.

Mr. McInturff insisted the boots found in a culvert four days after Bowen's arrest should have been found earlier and the gun in Chadwell Pond was not a reliable find . He maintained that Eva Ketron, who testified she seen Freddie throw the gun in the pond was standing 250 feet away, which is too far to be a reliable witness. He also brought up if Freddie had been wearing the boots the day he killed Betty then footprints should have been found. Nothing was found except for one footprint. Even the pants that Freddie had been wearing were never found. Are those pants also at the bottom of Chadwell Pond, did Freddie burn or bury them or could it be they were tossed into the outdoor toilet on the Laforce/Dunn property? Did the police dig through the bottom of an outdoor toilet?

McInturff even turned his accusations to Phillip Laforce since he had also been picked up and questioned in the murder and told the police that Bowen told him that "he killed somebody". Mr. McIntuff was told by Laforce that "everybody said he (Phillip Laforce) did it" when he was being questioned. It was common procedure that Mr. McInturff was followed by bringing up these things because he was trying to save the life of his client. The one thing I agree is Mr. McIntuff said that Bowen could not have committed the murder by himself because he only returned home only 45 minutes after the girl disappeared. I have gone through the court transcripts and logically if you look at the timeline and taking into the mechanics of what was done to Betty, the one question many have maintained is the time factor just doesn't add up with only one person being responsible. Also, how does one man while

157

holding a gun bind and gag a young 12 year old girl fighting for

her life?

McInturff asked for the sentencing to be withheld at the time

denied, the Court advised they had to follow procedure of

pronouncing judgment and sentence on a jury verdict.

Judgment was pronounced and he was sentenced to death by

electrocution that would occur on the 26th day of April 1971, three

days after his 27th birthday. Fred was told after sentence was

passed that he was allowed thirty days to move for a new trial if he

wanted a new trial.

A motion for a new trial was entered on September 4, 1970- Mr.

McInturff put witnesses on for Fred Bowen they were Sandra

Bowen and John Bishop. John Bishop was called on behalf of the

defendant and confirmed that he was one of the investigators for

the trial and he was employed by the Sheriff's Department. He

confirmed that he searched the property that Fred Bowen was

residing when he was arrested. He was asked if he found and took

into custody a pair of trousers which he confirmed. Two pair of

trousers was taken from the residence and one from Fred when he was arrested. A pair of brown trousers was found in the back bedroom of Rose Dunn's house with another pair of trousers. Sandra Bowen was then called to the stand and she was shown the trousers. She told the court he had a pair of trousers like the ones she was shown so they probably belonged to him.

Also brought up was testimony made by Phillip Laforce which indicated that he was given a lie detector test; however the results of the test could not be introduced. The results of the test could be in error since the Court restricted the results as evidence.

On September 4, 1970 Bowen was refused a new trial, Judge Byers said there was no grounds for the new trial and it was recommended that Bowen be taken immediately to prison from the solitary confinement cell he has been staying in since the night of his arrest.

After the Trial

On Sunday, July 26, 1970, the Kingsport Times News published a letter to the editor titled "What Made Freddie Tick?" who was written by a former resident of Kingsport that had moved to California.

Her letter started off with a request for the editor to publish her letter in full because to shorten it would not bring the full understanding to its reader. First she started out with her sympathy going out to the Necessary family over their loss and she explained that she knew Freddie Bowen and the trials and tribulations of his life. According to the writer of the letter, she had been connected with a business in Bloomingdale that put her in contact with the majority of school children at Kingsley Elementary and Ketron High School and working with the PTA.

She commended school Principal Glen Rowland that had tried his best to help Freddie Bowen and encourage him to stay in school. She pointed out that Freddie was raised by a mother that had little to live on and would not discipline him for anything. You could see Freddie at any hour of the day or night picking up pop bottles so he could turn them in for money.

Freddie could not be in closed quarters and climbed out a window when a teacher would not let him out the door. She also pointed out that Freddie got no education past the 4th grade and was socially promoted up to the 8th grade at which time he attended Ketron High School for a few days and then went back to Kingsley Elementary.

Freddie had a bad speech defect and was made fun of because of this. He could not be dared to do anything because he would take any dare. He had broken in the school and the boys that dared him would stand outside to help him eat what he had stolen. She also pointed out that Freddie was not one to lie about what he had done, instead he would brag.

One interesting fact, she pointed out was that Freddie was a violent man because she had seen him take a knife or broken bottle and try his best to kill people who made fun of his speech, his clothes or when they tried to take his bike which was his only prized possession.

You could tell Freddie all day to do something and he wouldn't do it, but all you would have to do is to ask him to do something and he would break his back to help you.

Freddie had half-brothers however, according to the writer of this letter his half-brothers did nothing for him and didn't want him to bother them.

She wanted to know how come the newspaper didn't tell the readers during his trial about him being a "little retarded" since he could not be held responsible for what he did?

She finished her letter with hopes the now grown up boys of Bloomingdale could sleep nights when they caused Freddie to do the things he did; when they dared him to ask a girl out and then stand back to laugh when the girl would turn him down. How did they feel about the times they would pour garbage or a soft drink on his bike, mocking him when he talked?

She commented at the end of the letter she didn't feel that Freddie was all to blame for what he had done and that a few more should have to stand up there in court with him.

Although I could never excuse Freddie for the crime he committed you can see from the description of him in her letter that Freddie was holding a lot of hurt and humiliation himself.

Rape as we all know is not a crime of passion, but a crime involving power and to dominate and show violence. It is truly a hate crime in every way possible.

Betty Necessary took the brunt of all of Freddie's hardships in life and paid the ultimate price.

I have always felt it strange that if Freddie would pick somebody to pay for what others had to do to him why did he pick Betty Necessary to pay for his hardships? The Necessary family was not rich, the family was poor, she was somebody that would never make fun of anybody and was quiet and shy, and she would help anybody because she had a heart of gold. Since Freddie Bowen would never admit to his crime and died confessing nothing to do with Betty Necessary's murder we will never know why or if this could have been stopped.

Freddie's Special Trip to Prison

Fred J. Bowen was the most hated man in Kingsport and the one thing that must be pointed out is the hostility in Bloomingdale against Freddie Bowen after his sentence was passed is still to this day well known. Bowen never asked to be released on bond and he did this for a reason.

A group of men assembled and had planned to abduct Freddie to hang him from the football goal post at the Ketron High School. These well-meaning men wanted to make sure that Freddie paid for his crime, but unfortunately could not take out their plans. Freddie's ride to prison was also an interesting since the sheriff's cruiser transporting him to Nashville was boxed between two cars. The two officers noticed that a white Ford was tailing them near Blaine 70 miles west of Kingsport then a GTO went around the cruiser at speeds they approximated to be between 80 to 90 miles per hour in a no passing zone. The GTO cut off sharply in front of the police cruiser and then slowed down at the same time the Ford pulled up against the cruiser bumper. When the officer driving tried to pull around the GTO it swerved out to block him. He could get out of the boxed position when he drove on the right shoulder of the road and passed both the GTO and the school bus beside it. Eventually the GTO got boxed in by heavy traffic; however the Ford continued to follow the cruiser until the Knoxville police were contacted ahead of time by radio and stopped the Ford. When the Knoxville police searched the Ford car they found weapons; however, since there was no record of any charges against the driver in Knoxville and they could not prove of a plot to harm Bowen so they were released. The identity of either driver has never been released to the public. Bowen appeared to be scared and shaken up during the incident.

Fred tried to get a new trial before his execution date getting closer and closer.

If Fred worried about being executed, he spent time wasted because in February 1971 Governor Winfield Dunn would allow no more executions until after the United States Supreme Court ruled on the constitutionality of the death penalty.

In June 1972 the U.S. Supreme Court decided the death penalty constituted cruel and inhuman punishment. Including Fred Bowen,

21 Tennessee death row inmates had their death sentence commuted to 99 year terms because of the Supreme Court decision. This would provide him for parole in 12 ½ years and even if the Death Penalty were reinstated it wouldn't do any good because it could not be overturned again. It was bad enough that Betty lost her life because of the monster like Fred Bowen now she was being raped all over again by the State of Tennessee.

In January 1973 Fred Bowen once again returned to Sullivan County to demand his release from prison by claiming that his attorneys had failed to call two witnesses that would prove he was innocent in the murder of Betty Necessary. During his return, he was barely recognizable since he had gained at least 20 pounds, mostly in his midsection and his hair had grown long and unkempt. The man who proclaimed that he loved cowboy boots and cowboy shirts came into court wearing blue jeans and a wrinkled blue denim shirt.

Fred claimed in court that his attorney's did not permit his half-brother, Andrew Bowen and his half-nephew, Donnie Bowen from testifying that he was with Donnie while Betty Necessary was abducted and slain. According to Burkett McInturff, Fred's attorney, he interviewed Andrew and Donnie Bowen and they wanted to help Freddie, but realized that a serious crime had been committed and they didn't want to get involved in trying to possibly cover up anything. Fred's attorneys had decided not to put Donnie or Andrew Bowen on the stand because of conflicting stories of what happened on the day of the murder. Donnie Bowen testified that he and Freddie had left Bloomingdale about 3:45pm the day of the murder and drove to a downtown jewelry store and returned after 5:00pm. Donnie was asked about a statement where he had signed earlier before Fred's first trial that indicated he left Fred at about 4:40pm at which time Donnie advised he was threatened by the TBI agent to sign it. Both Andrew and Donnie indicated they made a mistake earlier when asked about being in Johnson City on the day that Betty Jean was abducted; and claimed they were in Johnson City the day before this occurred. Once again, Fred was denied his freedom and returned to prison where he now made his home.

On December 24, 1974, Fred was stabbed by a fellow inmate 23 times with a homemade knife. When he was stabbed they also found a homemade knife on Fred which he used to put a cut on his assailant's hand. Later on it was discovered the assailant was Billy Joe White, who was not a cellmate. Mr. White was being held for questioning regarding the stabbing of Fred Bowen but he wasn't talking.

The bleeding from Fred's wounds was so bad he was not expected to live. A prison chaplain telephoned one of Fred's relatives in Kingsport to let him know that chances were he would not make it to the hospital since the injuries was so bad.

Bowen made it through and was questioned in the hospital, he told the warden he didn't know who stabbed him and wouldn't prosecute if he knew. According to the warden, Bowen has not been in trouble at the prison since his arrival and has stayed the last year in solitary confinement.

Fred Bowen tried often for a retrial and every time he came back to Sullivan County he looked less and less like the Fred Bowen that had killed Betty Jean Necessary. Fred was showing the signs of what happens when you live life the hard way in prison. The once slender, well groomed, dark headed young man turned into a sickly, messed up and over weight man that looked a great deal older than his actual years.

No matter how often Fred tried to get out of prison, the citizens of Kingsport and especially those in Bloomingdale never forgot what he did to Betty so petitions were signed to help keep him where he belonged. Betty's family fought hard to keep Fred in prison because they could never bear to relive what happened to her. The Necessary family never recovered fully from Betty's death and I don't know how you could recover from such a violent act. Not only did he kill their sister, he also denied ever killing Betty and showed no signs of remorse when he was eligible for parole. An article in the Kingsport Times News on May 19, 1998 set the tone for the most chilling of all facts pertaining to Fred's death sentence being overturned. Had Fred Bowen lived, he was to be released from prison, whether or not he was paroled in 2014 and possibly earlier for good behavior simply because his sentence was expiring. A race was run and time was running out. There was nothing that would ever bring Betty back, but if Fred Bowen was

ever released from prison, he would kill again and Betty knew this.

A Killer's Side of the Story

Suppose we look at another side of the story regarding the murder of Betty Jean Necessary. This in no way justifies what happened to her only to look at the killer's side of the story. Keep an open mind and try to learn from another possible perspective.

The following is a conversation between the author of this book and Fred J. Bowen. The wording was not changed and was written exactly as possible from the conversation.

The man in front of me hardly resembled a killer, he just looked like an old man that had smoked cigarettes all his life, his tar stained finger tips gave this away. He looked like one of those men your mother told you to stay away from and to avoid eye contact. The way he put his words and sentences together was a sad sign of how he had little formal education, even at the most elementary level and how he had been failed by the education system. But I wasn't there to judge his education, or lack thereof, I was there to listen to his side of the story and not to judge.

"Finally, after a long silence, he spoke - you want to hear my side of the story well here it is. I were up on top of that hill playing cards and drinking corn liquor. We played for money and I went up to get my money that I were owed. Her pappy was there with one of his girls and he didn't like the way I was looking at her so he told me to leave.

All I was up there for was to get my money owed to me, but he just looked at me and laughed. He told me he didn't owe me anything and to leave and not come back. Before I left I told him one way or the other I was going to get my money he owned me and he just laughed at me. I got mad because I don't like people to laugh at me 'cause I've been laughed at all my life.

The girl that got grabbed were not the same one that was up on the hill with her pappy that day. I guess I did kill that girl Betty but I were not the only one involved and I tried to tell them. There were other ones involved one of them was somebody that she knew and had no fear of, she didn't have any reason to be scared of him. This other feller involved were somebody I know real well and he were a lot like me- that is nobody wanted to be around him and I considered him to be a friend". So it sounded like he was telling

173

me he wasn't the only one involved so who else was involved in this?

"I only wanted to scare her pappy and make my point about the money, but things just got out of hand and before I knew it she were hurt. If I could take it back, what happened, I would".

Looking at the man in front of me, I could see where years of a hard life, a prison life, had beaten him down, but I could also see how that maybe in a different time in different circumstances, his life could have been better.

Freddie continued to talk and wanted to tell me about his niece, "she were a flirt he told me. She was all the time sitting on his lap trying to entice him and then one day something happened, but after he talked with his kin, they understood and dropped the charges".

Something told me there was more to Freddie Bowen than the murder of Betty Necessary and it was obvious he was hiding information about the other killer's involved with this crime. The others were never brought to justice and that was a crime wasn't it?

This probably explains why it was never covered in court or the newspapers why that a man living in Indiana for several months came in with his wife and for no reason "grabbed" a child he had never met from the roadway on her way home from school. How did he know she would be there? The road that Betty Necessary was grabbed from was not a well-traveled roadway where you could easily see walkers. In everybody's own words you couldn't see anybody after they got past a curve in the hill. What did he do, did he stalk her or did he know that she would travel up that hill-how could he have known that? How did he know how long it would take her to walk from the school to her friend's house, it was anybody's guess how long she would stay- she could have stayed for hours- but how did he know when to meet her or that she would even be there at the top of the hill?

The only possible solution was that he had at least one accomplice to help him. This could have easily been Fred's own brother in law often seen with a two way radio talking into it. How hard would it have been to watch a 12 year old girl in an area where no violence had ever taken place, on her way home from school?

Fred knew he would die in prison, so why would he not tell the truth about this?

Fred is Dead

The same newspaper that ran an article on February 27, 1970, the day after Betty Jean Necessary was abducted was running an article on March 1, 2006 which closed the chapter on a long book when it informed the readers that Betty's killer died in a Nashville hospital. Fred J. Bowen died from natural causes, which was the cancer that had been consuming his body for several years on February 26, 2006 this was exactly 36 years to the day he abducted his victim Betty Jean Necessary. The picture in the paper of Fred J. Bowen would bear little resemblance to the picture that Kingsport Times News had of Fred Bowen in 1970 after his arrest. No matter what, Betty had the last word and when he died the last thing he seen as he was taking his last painful breath was the face of a young, 12 year old Betty. This time when he saw her, she was without the gags and bindings he used on her and she could finally ask him the question we would all like to ask- why?

I can only hope this time she got her answer before the flames claimed his soul- it was finally time for payback and for Betty to see justice finally done.

Other Victims and Information of Interest

Anytime somebody is arrested for murder it reopens the possibility that another unsolved murder can be solved. During the trial of Fred Bowen the Kingsport Times newspaper reported that when Fred Bowen was being investigated for the murder of Betty Necessary he was also a prime suspect in not only two murders in Tennessee but also Kentucky and Florida.

Let's first point out that Fred was never indicted for the crimes mentioned, but with the possibility there is always the hope it will reopen a cold case that will bring resolution to a family. Cold cases are cases, frozen in time, unsolved, but far from forgotten, especially for the families and friends of the victims.

During the writing of this book, newspaper articles were found along with a letter dated March 6, 1970 to Sheriff Bill Wright with Sullivan County Sheriff's Department. The letter was written by Carl Kirkpatrick, District Attorney General.

This letter explains that General Kirkpatrick was informed that two detectives from Nashville, Tennessee came to the Sullivan County Jail and requested permission to interview Fred Bowen concerning other cases possibly against Mr. Bowen in Davidson County, Tennessee. It was requested the investigators involved in Sullivan County not let Mr. Bowen be interviewed by anyone without the consent of his attorneys. Somehow there was a request earlier and it was not honored which resulted in Fred being interviewed anyway by the men from Davidson County, Tennessee with the Sheriff's permission.

The purpose of the request was to let them know to not allow any other visitors to see him (other than family and attorneys) since it could seriously jeopardize the effectiveness of the prosecution for the charge he is in jail for which was Betty Necessary.

More interesting is a letter dated June 11, 1970 from the Office of District Attorney-General in Davidson County, Nashville, Tennessee to Carl Kirkpatrick. It is signed by Robert Brandt which was the Assistant District Attorney regarding Fred Bowen. The letter says in part that someone from their office may want to sit in on his trial since Fred Bowen was the prime suspect in a similar case in that area (Nashville).

Glenda Marie Sirmans was an eighth grader at Farragut

Elementary School in Knoxville and was described as shy but

happy. Glenda was 5 foot tall, 80 lbs., and 13 years old. A shy girl

in nature, very studious and was hard to get to know, but held dear

to her close friends and family which included two sisters and one

brother.

Glenda wouldn't talk to a new person very much until she got to

know them. But after she got to know them, she became a great

friend. At the time of her disappearance, she was working on a

school project with another schoolmate and walked to their house

which normally would take about 20 minutes at the most since it

was about a mile from her home.

The young girl left her home at approximately 3:30pm on

Saturday, November 29, 1969 and was walking toward the

schoolmate's house. When Glenda did not arrive at the home of

her friend they telephoned her parents at about 5:00pm to find out

why she had not arrived.

The last time Glenda was seen she was wearing a pink and a blue

jumper with a pink shirt underneath and pink hose. She was also wearing a green plaid coat with a fur collar which complimented the petite brunette's hair.

A shaggy black and white dog led the investigation of Glenda's body when he brought her shoe with the foot still inside to a nearby house. This led to the discovery of her remains on a hillside thick with trees and underbrush about 7 miles from her home on December 14th at about noon. According to the investigators the murder more than likely took place in the area where her body was found.

A foot path led from the nearby home where the dog carried the shoe with the foot and Deputy Fred Sheppard walked to the top of the rise of the hill and spotted a tree with a green plaid coat turned inside out at the base of the tree. In a thicket downhill from the coat was a nude body lying on leaves and pine needles. The scene was described by Deputy Fred Sheppard as the worst thing he has ever seen.

What was thought to be the body of the victim was only part of the body- from the waist down. The neck and torso of the victim had slash and stab marks. The condition of the body and exposure to the elements and animals made it impossible to determine if the victim was raped or sexually molested. Bits of cloth, bone and wads of human hair scattered on the hillside. Glenda had put up a vigilant fight for her life evidenced with her broken nails and hair pulled out by the roots.

The 20 acre patch of woods, she was found on was bordered by 3 roads which during the warm months would be the "lover's lane" of the area. The closest house in the area was about 400 yards and this was too far away to hear any noise.

The body of Glenda Sirmans was transported to Blount County Memorial Hospital which is close to Maryville for an autopsy.

On Friday following the investigation of the body a bone handled switch blade type pocket knife was discovered beside one of the roads that bordered the land where the body was discovered, but nothing could be found out about the owner of the knife and it was not reported if any blood was found on the knife.

Another unsolved murder that investigators wanted to question Fred Bowen about was the unsolved case of Kathy Jones in Nashville, Tennessee.

Kathy Jones, born Nora Kathylene Jones, a shy and religious 12 year old girl left her home from Lutie Street in Nashville, Tennessee, to go roller skating at around 7:45pm on November 29, 1969. The walk to the Thompson Street Roller Drome was only about a 20 minute walk from her house. Before she left her mother Nora gave her a dollar so she could stop at Krispy Kreme and get a donut and have a little spending money. Kathy thanked her mother and kissed her then she started out walking for the roller drome. Kathy had with her a used pair of roller skates that her cousin gave her; however, to Kathy it didn't matter they were used. The skates were Kathy's most prized possession. Kathy didn't arrive at the roller rink and she didn't go by the Krispy Kreme to get something to eat. It is hard to tell what exactly happened to Kathy but what is known is that her battered corpse was found by a civil service worker on December 2nd. Kathy's naked body was in high weeds, not far from a nearby house.

The body was on its side with the back bent, arms tied behind her back with a plaid cloth. Sightless eyes were slightly open with the head pushed far back, which exposed a blouse tied around the neck and mouth. Several almond shaped cuts were found on the throat of the victim and a puncture wound was below the small left breast. There was blood here and there, probably less than what one would expect for such a vicious act. The right leg of the victim was straight with the left knee drawn almost to the waist. The victim had been attacked both vaginally and anally. Both buttocks showed the brutality of this crime since both were black with bruising.

Clothes not used to bind the victim were crumpled beside her body. Estimated time of death was around 36 hours after she left her home, according to the police, which made the young girl's death more than likely on December 1st and her body was found December 2nd.

Newspaper articles never reported autopsy results of the Kathy Jones case; however, I found a much later article that mentioned they weren't equipped to do an autopsy at the time. The pictures and testimony of the police officers are the only thing that could point to the condition of the body.

Surprisingly Kathy did not die as the results of the wounds on her body, but from one of her own wadded up bobby socks which had been used as a gag that was so far down in her throat the mortician found it when she was being embalmed. This is something that even the police didn't find. Speculation is that when Kathy heard a voice she tried to cry out to get the attention of somebody; however her one last act to help herself proved fatal when she choked on her bobby sock when it became lodged and blocked her airway.

Since that time several people have been questioned regarding this matter, but no arrests have been made and the case is still cold. Other murders mentioned that Fred possibly had something to do with were in Pompano Beach, Florida, which is entirely possible since he had family ties in that area. After I searched murders of missing children in that area I came up with Jody Wells (11), who went missing from Jacksonville on August 30, 1969.

Jody was found in a secluded wooded area shot 4 times in the back, she had been hidden under broken branches in an advanced stage of decomposition. This case is still unsolved even though several people were questioned.

On June 2, 1969 the body of a young woman was found in Harlan, Kentucky about 50 feet off the Little Shepard area which is a rural area on top of Pine Mountain, Kentucky State Route 1679. She was estimated to be from late teens to mid 20's, however you have to allow the possibility either way on the age range since looks can deceive. The young woman had medium length light brown or even strawberry blonde hair dyed auburn in places. She was medium in build, but her true weight couldn't be determined since decomposition was too advanced. Her height was determined to be around 5'3". The date she had been killed was more than likely in May of 1969, but her estimated time of death could have been as far back as 12 weeks longer than anticipated. Whether or not she was raped also could not be determined due to decomposition being advanced. Identifying marks were scars on her legs, she had a burn mark about ¾ inches wide on her right leg midway down between the knee and thigh. The scar was on the outside of the leg and followed down the backside of the leg. There was also a scar three inches above the right knee on the outside of the knee, which was around 1 ½ inches long with two clamp marks. There was also a scar about three inches long below and beside the clamp scar mentioned. The police believed that it was possible the victim was from or had been visiting the Cincinnati, Ohio area since a ticket stub from a restaurant in Cincinnati was found near the body. There was nothing else found close to the body that would help point where the victim had been from but it was believed that the victim had been murdered elsewhere and dumped at the remote location where she was found. Despite the advanced state of decomposition the local funeral home could conduct an open casket service in hopes she could be identified and even though the local police viewed the body she was never identified so it was assumed that more than likely she was not from the area. In 2014 this case was reopened and the body was exhumed to obtain DNA and maybe identify her.

This victim needs her rightful name given back to her; she need not lie at the bottom of a grave with a headstone on top of her that reads Jane Doe. She is not Jane Doe she is somebody, a daughter, a sister, a friend, but more than anything she is somebody. I don't know that Fred killed this person it could have been him as much as it could have been anybody else. I would urge anybody that knows anything to talk to the authorities.

I tried to talk to Fred's ex-wife Sandra LaForce Bowen and get more information about Fred's whereabouts and the possibility of his involvement in these crimes or even other possible crimes. In no way did I want to point a finger at Sandra or even to ask her how she could be married Fred Bowen but considered her to be a victim and all the other people he had hurt but she would never talk to me. Maybe if the Knoxville or Nashville police had spoken to her when Fred was arrested for Betty Necessary's murder we may have more information on the possibility on his involvement of these crimes but that is probably something that we will never know. My interest was not to help write this book, but to bring justice and closure to the victims. There can be nothing worse than never finding out who killed your loved one and being brought to justice.

Final Words

We owe these victims one thing which is justice. I urge anybody that knows anything about these or any other murders to come forward.

The crime of murder has no statute of limitations.

BIOGRAPHIES

Carl Kirkpatrick was born in Kingsport; he was a graduate of Vanderbilt University. Mr. Kirkpatrick was a District Attorney General in Sullivan County, for Tennessee's 2nd Judicial District for 28 years working on over 15,000 cases. After retirement from Sullivan County he became a U.S. Federal Prosecutor in Knoxville, Tennessee.

Judge John Byers an East Tennessee native, graduated from ETSU and was also a University of Tennessee graduate. Judge Byers practiced law for several years. After the Bowen trial Judge Byers was accused by Fred Bowens' attorneys of erring due to not declaring the capital punishment cruel and inhumane.

James Keesling was born in Smyth County, Virginia in 1933; he was a graduate of ETSU and the FBI National Academy. He worked at Bristol Virginia Police Department and afterwards Tennessee Bureau of Investigation where he retired as Assistant Director and became Police Chief of Kingsport Police Department in the mid 1980's where he worked until his retirement in 2000.

Burkett McInturff was a graduate of Cumberland University School of Law and his career spanned over 65 years. Lawyer McInturff as Burkett liked to be called was appointed with Shelburne Ferguson to represent Freddie Bowen in the Betty Necessary case. Burkett was the go to attorney for anyone in trouble and since he was appointed in this case he made little money, but got a great deal of exposure in the newspapers and media. Burkett said that he would give his clients a million dollar defense for a fraction of the cost. For more information on Burkett McInturff read the books by J.S. Moore Picking Strawberries: The Burkett McInturff Story and The Big Mac Book.

Shelburne Ferguson had only been out of college for 5 years when he joined Burkett McInturff in representing Freddie Bowen. He is a graduate of the University of Tennessee and still practices law in Kingsport, Tennessee.

Edgar Calhoun received his law degree from the University of Tennessee and worked for Kingsport Times News about 5 years as a reporter and sports editor before working for the Sullivan County Attorney District Attorney General's Office as a Prosecutor. He was elected judge for 16 years.

Sheriff Bill Wright was elected as Sheriff in Sullivan County in 1966. He formerly worked at the City of Kingsport Police Department as a detective for over 10 years. In 1971 accusations were made against the Sheriff's Department one of the complaints concerned Freddie Bowen's incarceration in the jail during the trail for Betty Necessary. According to local newspapers prisoners in the jail could squirt lighter fluid on Bowen and throw lit matches on him. The allegations were unfounded.

John Bishop at the time of the Necessary murder was an investigator, but later became Sheriff in 1972. In January 1973 Mr. Bishop and his family were burned out of their home when he led a gambling raid from local clubs, and gambling machine repair shops..

My Personal Thanks

Without the continual support of my husband, Dale Farmer, I could never have completed this project; he has always been there for me.

J.S. Moore- you taught me I could do this and encouraged me to be honest with myself.

My parents, Dale and Arda Ford- without you I wouldn't be here- my only regret is that Dad was not around to read my book when complete.

Wanda & Joyce Hickman, Kathy Elliott Davidson and other friends of Betty- your courage will be rewarded in life, thank you so much for being kind to Betty and being kind to her memory.

Chief Keesling, District Attorney's Office, City of Kingsport Police Department and Darla Anderson- your kindness and dedication and assistance and insight helped so much with the writing of this book; I could never thank you enough.

Misty Davis- my sister and Mary Jane Farmer and Debbie Farmer- my sister's in law, Peggy Farmer- my mother in law. All these ladies were my proof readers and my cheerleaders.

Bob Bonwit- for your medical knowledge; thank you so much for helping me understand medical reports and terminology.

Becky Campbell- thank you for helping find old newspaper articles.

Wanda and Ralph Fields- for showing me the location of the cave and surrounding.

Kingsport Times News- for newspaper articles, pictures and drawings regarding the case.

Mariann Collette, Ethel Crites and Elaine Watson for your spiritual guidance.

Photo by Cyndee Webb Photography
Cover design by Kathy Snapp

Photographs and Articles

VOLUME LIX, No. 41   KINGSPORT, TENNESSEE, 37660, FRIDAY, FEB. 27, 1970   3 SECTIONS   30 PAGES   10 CENTS ☆

FAMILY WAITS at home while officers search for missing Kingsley School student, Betty Jean Necessary, 12. From left: Mrs. Dorothy Necessary, Teresa, Bill, and Walter. (Times-News Photo—Charles Dean)

The newspaper article that announced Betty was missing

199

The cave, as pictured in February 1970

'YOU BURIED HER WHILE
SHE WAS STILL ALIVE'

Only the person who killed Betty Jean Necessary really knows what happened between the time she was seen walking toward a lonesome curve and the time her body was found in a shallow grave.

But Friday, District Attorney Carl Kirkpatrick electrified a packed courtroom during a dramatic account of the state's view of events that winter day.

It came when Fred J. Bowen took the witness stand to deny the murder:

"You walked up to that cave," Kirkpatrick told him, "and planned how you'd get that little girl. You'd seen her before, and you took off your tee shirt and ripped it up to be ready . . .

"And when you saw her walking up that road by herself, you knew you had your chance . . .

"And when she walked into those woods it was you behind her with a gun in her back. And when she got scared and threw down her books and ran, you hit her in the head with that gun and made her walk to where the clothes were found . . .

"And then you tied her and gagged her and ripped off her clothes and raped her on the spot . . .

"And then you put that coat over her shoulders and walked her to the cave. And then you shot her in the front and she fell to her knees. And then you pumped four slugs into her back while she was still on her hands and knees . . .

"And then you buried her while she was still alive."

201

House Blurred for Privacy

Curve in the road as it appears today

SUMMARY COMMENT:

Five gunshot wound are demonstrated, four of which enter the back of the chest, and one in the right lower abdomen. Three of the bullet tracts penetrate the lungs and the cause of death is hemorrhage from both lungs into the pleural cavities. The time of death is probably not long after disappearance on February 26. There is moderate post mortem decomposition but in view of the cold temperatures in the interval natural refrigeration probably retarded this process. The fact that she is known to have had a luncheon at approximately noon and disappeared at approximately 4 p.m. and the fact that there is a digested meal still present in the stomach would indicate that death occurred probably not long after she was last seen. The postmortem decomposition indicates that the body had been exposed even at the cold temperatures for at least 48 hours. There is evidence of rape in the tearing of the fourchet and strongly positive acid phosphatase in the vaginal secretion.

Final Results of Autopsy

203

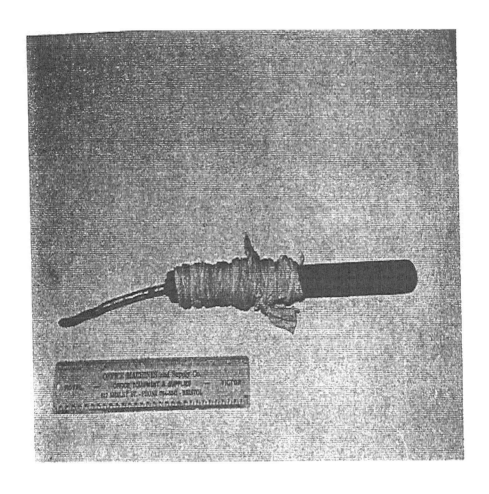

Weapon Used in Murder

Department of Public Safety
Division of Police
1000 East Center Street
Kingsport, Tennessee

11795

Date: 2-28-70

Name Fred J Bowen

Address 946 N Temple Indianapolis, Ind.

Color-Sex White Male

Age 25

Birthdate and Place 4-23-44 St. Charles, VA.

Height-Weight 13' 150 LBS.

Hair-Eyes Bro Hair Blue Eyes

Military-Serial No. None

Social Security No.

Relatives

Name	Address	Relation
Sandy Bowen	946 N Temple Indianapolis Ind	Wife
Charles	— — —	Bro.
Andrew	— 3011 Bloomingdale	Half Bro.

Driver's License No. and State

Automobile Info 66 Pontiac Boneville 61 Cadillac

Associates

Occupation Unemployed (Formerly Standard Brand Indianapolis, Ind)

Employment

Education

Scars and Marks Scars on Right Arm at Elbow

Criminal Record 1st. Degree Murder 2-28-70

Fingerprints of the killer Fred Bowen

Picture of killer Freddie J. Bowen

EXECUTIVE ASSISTANT
DISTRICT-ATTORNEY
GENERAL

ROBERT S. BRANDT

ASSISTANT DISTRICT
ATTORNEYS-GENERAL

KENT SANDIDGE, III
J. RANDALL WYATT, JR.
ALBERT D. NOE, IV
CARLTON H. PETWAY
HAROLD D. HARDIN
RICHARD P. McCULLY
C. DOUGLAS THORESEN
MARTHA CRAIG DAUGHTREY

OFFICE OF DISTRICT ATTORNEY-GENERAL

607 METROPOLITAN COURTHOUSE
NASHVILLE, TENNESSEE 37201

TENTH JUDICIAL CIRCUIT
DAVIDSON COUNTY

DISTRICT ATTORNEY GENERAL
THOMAS H. SHRIVER

CHIEF INVESTIGATOR
CHARLES M. HUNTER

INVESTIGATORS
STERLING P. GRAY
JIMMIE A. SELLS
BILLY W. WATKINS

ADMINISTRATIVE ASSISTANT
MRS. PAULINE B. WEHBY

June 11, 1970

Honorable Carl Kirkpatrick
District Attorney General
Sullivan County Courthouse
Blountville, Tennessee

Re: State vs. Freddie Bowen

Dear Carl:

I learned today from one of your assistants that the above styled case is set for trial on July 20, 1970. As I am sure you are aware, the defendant in your case is a prime suspect in a similar case here. It may be that someone from this office will want to sit in on his trial. Please keep us posted if there is any continuance in this case.

Yours truly,

Robert S. Brandt
Assistant District Attorney

RSB:ps

cc: file

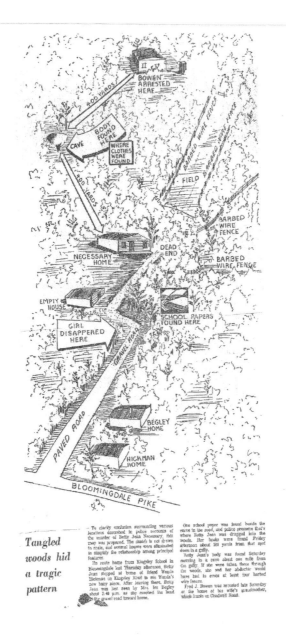

Tangled woods hid a tragic pattern

To clarify confusion surrounding various locations connected in police accounts of the murder of Betty Jean Necessary, this map was prepared. The sketch is not drawn to scale, and several houses were eliminated to simplify the relationship among principal features.

En route home from Kingsley School in Bloomingdale last Thursday afternoon, Betty Jean stopped at home of friend Wanda Hickman on Kingsley Road to see Wanda's new baby niece. After leaving there, Betty Jean was last seen by Mrs. Ira Begley about 2:40 p.m. as she reached the bend in the gravel road toward home.

One school paper was found beside the curve in the road, and police presume that's where Betty Jean was dragged into the woods. Her books were found Friday afternoon about 100 yards from that spot down in a gully.

Betty Jean's body was found Saturday morning in a cave about one mile from the gully. If she were taken there through the woods, she and her abductor would have had to cross at least four barbed wire fences.

Fred J. Bowen was arrested late Saturday at the home of his wife's grandmother, which stands on Chadwell Road.

Map of Betty Jean's Route

209

J. Edgar Hoover
Director.

The following FBI record, NUMBER   926 277 E   , is furnished FOR OFFICIAL USE ONLY.

CONTRIBUTOR OF FINGERPRINTS	NAME AND NUMBER	ARRESTED OR RECEIVED	CHARGE	DISPOSITION
SO Blountville Tenn	Freddy J Bowen #1850	1-28-63	B&E	2 to 3 yrs awaiting ci official sent
SO Miami Fla	Freddie J. Bowen #CR-81444	7-11-64	crim registration	rel immediately
PD Indianapolis Ind	Fred J Bowen #186715	8-30-66	drk CCW	
PD Indpls Ind	Fred J Bowen #186715	2-14-67	doc, pre rape cont to delin minor	NG no affid no affid
PD Kingsport Tenn	Fred J Bowen #11795	7-1-68	viol Registration Laws, no driv lic	fined $59.50 & $19.50
PD Kingsport Tenn	Fred J. Bowen #11795	2-28-70	1st degree murder	

Fred's record

Information shown on this Identification Record represents data furnished FBI by fingerprint contributors. Where final disposition is not shown or further explanation of charge is desired, communicate with agency contributing those fingerprints.
Notations indicated by * are NOT based on fingerprints in FBI files but are listed only as investigative leads as being possibly identical with subject of this record.   U.S. GOVERNMENT PRINTING OFFICE : 1943 O—557-691

Fred Bowen's Record

Search Launched For Missing Girl

Friday, Feb. 27

Child's killer dies in hospital in Nashville

■ **Freddie Bowen** was sentenced to death for killing 12-year-old Kingsport girl Betty Jean Necessary, but his sentence was later commuted to 99 years.

By BECKY CAMPBELL
bcampbell@timesnews.net

BOWEN

KINGSPORT — Thirty-six years to the day.

Feb. 26, 1970, Betty Jean Necessary died at the hands of Freddie Bowen.

Feb. 26, 2006, Bowen died in a Nashville hospital while serving a 99-year sentence for killing the 12-year-old girl.

Bowen, 61, died at 11 p.m. Sunday at Metro General Hospital of natural causes, according to Amanda Sluss, public information officer for the Tennessee Department of Correction.

Bowen had been incarcerated at the DeBerry Special Needs Facility since Sept. 9, Sluss said, and had been in and out of Metro General since that time.

"DeBerry is a hospital setting serving inmates with special medical or mental health needs," Sluss said.

Prior to being moved to DeBerry, Bowen was housed at Northwest Correctional Complex in Tiptonville, she said.

Sluss was prohibited by state law from revealing Bowen's medical condition, but Betty Jean Necessary's sister, Patty Powell, said Tuesday that she learned at a parole hearing last year that Bowen had cancer.

Powell and her family led a years-long crusade to keep Bowen in prison by getting area citizens to sign petitions opposing parole the four times he was eligible.

The day Betty Jean Necessary died was not much different from any other day — she went to school at Kingsley Elementary and then home with friends to the point they scattered to their respective homes.

The last gesture she made to two school friends that day

Please see CHILD'S, page 2A

In Memoriam

IN GOD'S OWN TIME

Not till the loom is silent
And the shuttles cease to fly
Will God unfold the canvass
And show the reason why.

The dark threads are as needful
In the skillful weaver's hand
As the threads of gold and silver
In the pattern that He planned.

A Sweet Memory printed in the Kingsley Annual

Made in the USA
Columbia, SC
05 August 2024

39605384R00117